Christian Ethics

Embodying Christian Values in Daily Decisions

by

Yesu Vi

Table of Contents

Introduction

In an ever-evolving world, where moral landscapes shift like sand underfoot, the quest for enduring principles to guide one's life has never been more pertinent. This quest transcends mere philosophical musing, touching the core of our existence and demanding a roadmap for navigating life's myriad complexities. For Christians, this roadmap is found not in the transient ideologies of our age but in the enduring truths of Scripture, interpreted and applied in the light of Christian moral principles.

The essence of Christian morality, with its rich tapestry woven from threads of ancient wisdom, scripture, and lived experience, presents not just rules for conduct but a vision for a fulfilled life. This vision, deeply rooted in love, faith, and hope, invites believers to transcend mere compliance, engaging with the world in transformative ways.

Yet, integrating Christian moral principles into the daily grind presents challenges. Life seldom offers us clear-cut decisions. More often, we navigate shades of gray, where the moral path is obscured by competing interests, complex relationships, and the pressures of contemporary life. In these moments, the wisdom of the ages, as preserved in scripture and tradition, becomes not just a lamp to our feet but a beacon in the fog.

This book seeks to serve as that beacon. It is crafted for those who yearn to apply Christian principles to decision-making processes, those who seek to embody virtue in every action, and for anyone who desires to explore the depth of Christian ethics beyond the surface level. Whether you are a long-time believer seeking to deepen your application of Christian principles, a theology student eager to explore the intersections of faith and ethics, a church leader guiding your community through moral decision-making, or an individual intrigued by moral philosophy, this book aims to meet you where you are.

Embarking on this journey, we begin by delving into the essence of Christian ethics, exploring its foundations and distinctions. Understanding that ethical living extends beyond knowing what is right and wrong—it requires a transformation of heart and mind, a cultivation of virtues that reflect the character of Christ.

Scripture and tradition offer a wealth of wisdom, providing not only ethical norms but also narratives that reveal the complexities of human nature and the grace of divine intervention. By engaging with these sources, we not only learn about moral principles but are also invited into a deeper relationship with the divine, a relationship that shapes and nurtures our moral compass.

Virtue ethics, rooted in character formation, challenges us to consider not just the ethics of action but the ethics of being. It invites us to pursue not merely the good life in a material sense but a life that is good in its essence, reflecting the goodness of God.

In the realm of decision-making, understanding God's will becomes a central concern. Discerning this will is not about deciphering a divine code but engaging in a relationship with God that illuminates our paths, guiding our choices in alignment with His purposes.

Issues of life and death, marriage and family, work and wealth, technology, social justice, tolerance, forgiveness, and the ethical implications of globalization are not merely topical concerns but arenas for the application of Christian ethics. Each realm offers unique challenges and opportunities for believers to bear witness to the transformative power of the gospel.

As we navigate these issues, we are called not to retreat from the world but to engage it with grace, conviction, and a deep sense of responsibility. This engagement is not passive but active, requiring us to make daily choices that reflect our commitment to Christ and His kingdom.

This book aims to inspire, challenge, and equip you to make those choices. Through a blend of expository clarity, motivational fervor, and inspirational depth, it seeks to guide you in weaving the principles of Christian ethics into the fabric of your daily life. In doing so, it aspires to provide not just knowledge but wisdom—the wisdom to live a life that is authentic, transformative, and deeply aligned with the eternal truths of the Christian faith.

As you turn these pages, may you find not only guidance for the journey but also nourishment for the soul. May the principles explored here illuminate your path, inspire your heart, and equip you to navigate life's complexities with grace, courage, and unwavering faith.

In closing, this introduction serves not as a comprehensive guide to Christian ethics but as an invitation—a call to journey deeper into understanding, applying, and living out the principles that define our faith. It is an invitation to explore how ancient wisdom speaks into contemporary issues, guiding us toward lives of integrity, compassion, and purpose. Welcome to this journey. May it be transformative, enlightening, and richly rewarding.

Chapter 1:
Understanding Christian Ethics

As we delve into the heart of Christian ethics, it's essential to embark on a journey of understanding the intricate blend of faith, hope, and love that forms the cornerstone of how we, as followers of Christ, make decisions that honor God and reflect His teachings in our daily lives. Christian ethics, far more than a set of rules, invites us into a deeper engagement with the divine wisdom and compassion found in Scripture. This initial chapter sets the stage for an exploration into the rich tapestry of moral philosophy rooted in Christian beliefs, integrating historical perspectives and the distinctiveness of Christian morality. At its core, Christian ethics is about aligning our lives with the moral foundations of faith, hope, and love—principles that not only guide us but also challenge us to live out our convictions authentically in a complex world. Here, we're not just learning to distinguish right from wrong but are also being equipped to navigate the multifaceted scenarios of life with grace and wisdom. This journey through Christian ethics is not just about absorbing knowledge; it's about transformation, about becoming beacons of light that reflect the profound love of Christ in every action we take and every decision we make.

Defining Christian Ethics

In the vast tapestry of moral philosophies, Christian ethics emerges as a distinctive thread, marked by its rootedness in the teachings and life of

Jesus Christ. Integrating these principles into the fabric of everyday life requires a deep understanding of what it means to live out one's faith amidst the complexities of the modern world. At its core, Christian ethics is concerned with how the redemptive work of Christ influences the moral and ethical decisions of His followers. It's not merely about adhering to a set of rules or guidelines, but about transforming the heart and mind to reflect Christ's love and righteousness in every action, thought, and decision.

Indeed, the beauty of Christian ethics lies in its ability to transcend time and culture, offering timeless truths that guide one's conduct. However, it also challenges believers to discern wisely, recognizing the contextual nuances of applying these truths in a rapidly changing world. Through the lens of Scripture, tradition, and reasoned faith, followers of Christ are invited to embark on a journey of moral and spiritual formation. This journey is not a solitary pursuit; it is done in community, inspired by the Holy Spirit, and with a view towards the flourishing of both individual and collective well-being. As we delve into defining Christian ethics, we lay the foundation to explore its application in a multitude of ethical decisions and dilemmas, always pointing back to the love and Lordship of Jesus Christ.

The Role of Scripture in Ethical Decision-Making

As we delve into the significance of scripture in guiding our moral compass, it's essential to connect its teachings with the fabric of our daily lives. Scripture isn't merely a collection of ancient texts detached from the present but a living, breathing guide that illuminates the path of righteousness in the complexities of modern existence.

The wisdom found within the Bible provides a foundation upon which believers can build their understanding of what it means to live a life that is pleasing to God. In moments of ethical dilemma, scripture acts not just as a point of reference but as a compass that points us towards the light, even when the way seems shrouded in darkness.

Scripture holds a privileged position in the process of ethical decision-making. Its role cannot be overstated; it serves as a direct link to divine wisdom, offering insights that transcend human understanding. This does not mean that the path it illuminates is always straightforward. The complexity of life's challenges often requires us to engage deeply with scripture, wrestling with its meanings and applications in our context.

One of the key aspects of utilizing scripture in ethical decision-making is the practice of discernment. Discernment is a process that involves prayerful reflection on the words of the Bible, inviting the Holy Spirit to guide our understanding and actions. It's a journey that asks believers to be both humble and courageous, open to being transformed by the truths discovered in scripture.

However, interpreting scripture in the context of ethical decision-making isn't merely an individual endeavor. It's a communal activity that benefits from the wisdom of the larger faith community. The body of Christ is equipped with diverse gifts, including the gift of teaching and discernment, which can provide invaluable insights into the complex moral issues of our time.

In navigating the waters of ethical decision-making, it's crucial to approach scripture with a heart of integrity. This means seeking not what we want the scripture to say but what it truly says. It involves putting aside personal biases and desires, allowing God's word to challenge and change us.

Scripture also offers us the narratives of individuals who faced ethical dilemmas and made choices that reflected their commitment to God. These stories are not just historical accounts but powerful examples of faith in action. They remind us that ethical living is not just about adhering to a set of rules but about embodying a relationship with God that transforms our actions.

It's equally important to recognize that scripture does not explicitly address every modern ethical dilemma we might face. In these instances, the principles of scripture offer a framework through which we can evaluate situations and make decisions. Love, justice, mercy, and humility are just a few of the scriptural principles that can inform our ethical choices.

Applying scripture to ethical decision-making also requires a commitment to ongoing learning and growth. As believers, our understanding of scripture deepens over time, influenced by study, prayer, and life experiences. This journey of understanding equips us to navigate the ethical challenges of life with wisdom and grace.

The role of scripture in ethical decision-making also underscores the importance of biblical literacy. Familiarity with the breadth and depth of scripture enriches our ability to draw upon its wisdom when faced with complex decisions. This knowledge enables us to respond to contemporary issues with insights grounded in eternal truths.

Moreover, engaging with scripture in the context of ethical decision-making fosters a sense of accountability. It reminds us that our choices are not just personal or private matters but are observed by God. This awareness can motivate believers to pursue what is right and good, even when it is difficult.

In the journey of ethical decision-making, scripture also offers comfort and hope. Its promises and assurances provide strength and resilience in the face of challenges, reminding believers that they do not navigate this path alone. God's presence and guidance are always available to those who seek Him through His word.

Ultimately, the role of scripture in ethical decision-making is transformative. By engaging with scripture, believers are shaped and molded into the image of Christ. This transformation impacts not just the individual but also the wider community, as ethical decisions made in alignment with scriptural principles contribute to the flourishing of society.

In conclusion, scripture is an indispensable guide in the journey of ethical decision-making. Its teachings, principles, and narratives provide a rich resource for navigating the moral complexities of life. As believers engage with scripture, they are equipped to make decisions that reflect God's heart, bringing light and life into the world.

Historical Perspectives

As we tread further into understanding Christian ethics, it's pivotal to anchor our insights in the rich soil of historical perspectives. The ethos of Christian morality didn't emerge in a vacuum but was cultivated through centuries of theological reflection, cultural interaction, and philosophical inquiry. The historical journey of Christian ethics showcases a tapestry woven with threads of change and continuity, reflecting the faith's adaptability and steadfastness.

In the earliest days of Christianity, the moral teachings of Jesus and his immediate followers set a radical new direction in a world accustomed to different moral standards. The Sermon on the Mount, with its beatitudes, offered a blueprint for living that contrasted sharply with prevailing societal norms. It wasn't merely a call to moral excellence but a redefinition of what moral excellence meant—centered on the heart rather than mere compliance with law.

As the early church grew, it grappled with integrating the teachings of Jesus into a cohesive ethical framework. This was no small feat in a Greco-Roman culture rich in philosophical traditions. Early Christian thinkers like Clement of Alexandria and Tertullian began to engage with and sometimes challenge these traditions, asserting the primacy of faith in guiding ethical behavior. They delineated a Christian morality that emphasized virtues such as faith, hope, and love, grounded in the belief of an imminent second coming of Christ.

The Constantinian shift, where Christianity transitioned from persecution to prominence within the Roman Empire, marked another pivotal moment in the evolution of Christian ethics. The fusion of church and state roles compelled Christian leaders to rethink aspects of moral teaching, particularly around issues of power, war, and wealth. St. Augustine's reflections on the City of God versus the City of Man navigated these complexities, offering insights on the interplay between earthly citizenship and heavenly allegiance.

Moving into the Middle Ages, Thomas Aquinas' synthesis of Christian theology and Aristotelian philosophy represented a significant milestone in the development of Christian ethics. Aquinas argued for natural law's consistency with divine revelation, positing that human reason could discern moral truths in harmony with biblical teaching. His work provided a comprehensive ethical system that influenced Christian thought profoundly.

The Reformation era introduced fresh perspectives on the relationship between faith and works, scripture, and church authority. Reformers like Martin Luther and John Calvin emphasized salvation by faith alone, challenging the ethical implications of traditional church teachings and practices. Their insistence on scripture as the ultimate authority in moral matters re-centered Christian ethics on biblical foundations, even as it provoked debates about interpretation and application.

In the modern era, the Enlightenment and the rise of individualism posed new challenges to Christian ethics. The emphasis on reason and autonomy led some to question the relevance of traditional moral teachings. Yet, this period also saw Christians like John Wesley engaging deeply with social ethics, advocating for justice and compassion in response to the industrial revolution's excesses.

The 20th century witnessed the emergence of liberation theology and the social gospel, highlighting the imperative of social justice in Christian ethics. These movements underscored the ethical mandate to address structural sins—poverty, racism, and sexism—and to work towards a more just and equitable society. They extended the application of Christian ethics beyond personal morality to systemic issues, challenging Christians to live out their faith in action.

In contemporary times, Christian ethics faces the task of navigating an increasingly pluralistic and technologically advanced world. Issues like bioethics, environmental stewardship, and digital ethics present new moral challenges. Here, the historical journey of Christian ethics serves as a reservoir of wisdom and insight, offering both caution and direction. It reminds us that while the contexts may change, the core principles of faith, hope, and love remain relevant anchors.

The historical perspectives of Christian ethics illuminate the faith's dynamic and responsive nature. They reveal a tradition that, while rooted in the teachings of Jesus and the apostolic church, has continually evolved in conversation with changing cultural, philosophical, and scientific landscapes. This historical journey underscores the adaptability of Christian ethics, its capacity to engage constructively with new moral challenges while holding fast to its foundational commitments.

In this light, studying the historical perspectives of Christian ethics is not an academic exercise in nostalgia. Rather, it's a vital practice for understanding how the faith has navigated moral dilemmas over millennia. It equips us with the intellectual humility to recognize that our current challenges are part of a larger, ongoing dialogue about how to live rightly before God and with each other.

Therefore, as we seek to apply Christian moral principles to our daily situations and decisions, let us do so with an appreciation of the historical journey that has shaped these principles. Let us draw on the rich wellspring of wisdom gleaned from centuries of faithful reflection and practice. Let this historical understanding embolden us to face contemporary ethical challenges with courage, creativity, and conviction, always striving to reflect the love and righteousness of Christ in a complex world.

Historical perspectives on Christian ethics thus serve as a beacon, guiding us through the tumultuous seas of moral complexity. They remind us that our efforts to live out Christian principles are part of a grand narrative that spans across generations. As we continue this journey, may we be inspired by those who have walked the path before us, forging a legacy of faith that seeks to understand and transform the world in the light of Christ's teachings. In this endeavor, may we find not only guidance but also hope, for in the history of Christian ethics, we see evidence of God's enduring presence, leading His people through every challenge toward His ultimate purposes of love and righteousness.

The Distinctiveness of Christian Morality

In the journey of exploring Christian ethics, it becomes evident that Christian morality holds a unique place in the vast expanse of moral philosophy. What sets it apart isn't just its historical roots or its sacred texts, but the very essence of its teachings, which invite a radical transformation of the heart and mind. At the core of Christian morality lie the profound principles of faith, hope, and love, principles that guide believers not just in what they should do, but fundamentally in who they are called to be. It's about a morality deeply intertwined with the individual's relationship with the divine, a path that invites one into a deeper understanding and practice of these virtues in every aspect of life. This distinctiveness is not to insulate but to inspire, not to separate but to engage with the world in a way that brings light to the darkness. As we delve deeper into the nuances of Christian ethics, we recognize that this moral vision challenges us to look beyond the letter of the law, to the spirit of love that underpins it, prompting a reflection on how we live out our faith, hope, and love in daily decisions and interactions.

Faith, Hope, and Love as Moral Foundations

In the journey of navigating life's complexities through a Christian lens, the principles of faith, hope, and love emerge not just as virtues but as foundational pillars for moral decision-making. At the heart of Christian ethics lies the profound understanding that these three elements are intertwined in the very fabric of our moral consciousness, guiding us toward a life that reflects the character of Christ.

The essence of faith, in its most fundamental form, is trust — a trust in the unseen, a firm belief in God's promises, and a steadfast reliance on the character of God. This trust is not passive; it's a dynamic force that propels us forward, influencing our choices and actions. When we ground our ethical decisions in faith, we are saying that, beyond human understanding and despite the uncertainty of outcomes, there is a greater plan orchestrated by a loving God. This reassurance allows us to navigate moral dilemmas with confidence, not in our own wisdom, but in the steadfastness of divine guidance.

Hope serves as the horizon for our journey, illuminating paths when our circumstances seem insurmountable. In a world brimming with cynicism and despair, hope offers a counter-narrative — one that insists on the possibility of a future defined not by our current struggles but by divine promises. It is this forward-looking optimism that shapes our moral vision, allowing us to engage with the world not as it is, but as it could be under the reign of God's justice and peace.

When our actions are rooted in hope, they bear the mark of expectation, working towards the Kingdom of God even amidst trials and tribulations.

Love, however, is perhaps the most compelling of the three, for it encapsulates the very nature of God. To act in love is to echo the sacrificial nature of Christ, who laid down His life out of love for humanity. This love is agape — selfless, unconditional, and active, seeking the good of the other before oneself. In the context of Christian ethics, love becomes the lens through which all actions are judged. It asks, "Does this decision reflect God's love? Will it bring about the greatest good for my neighbor?" When love guides our moral compass, our choices become not just good but godly, reflecting the heart of the Father.

The convergence of faith, hope, and love in ethical decision-making aligns us with the transformative power of the Gospel. Each decision informed by these virtues contributes to the unfolding of God's kingdom on earth, marking us as bearers of light in a landscape often dominated by shadows. The moral foundation they provide is both a gift and a task — a gift of divine guidance in our ethical journey, and a task to embody these virtues in every aspect of our lives.

Embedding faith, hope, and love into the fabric of our daily decisions challenges us to rise above the cultural ethos of individualism and self-gratification. It calls for a radical reorientation of our priorities, focusing on communal well-being and the flourishing of all creation. This is no small feat, yet the promise of divine assistance accompanies the challenge, empowering us to live out these principles in tangible, impactful ways.

In practice, faith calls us to confront ethical dilemmas with a posture of trust. Whether navigating complex work situations or personal relationships, faith informs our decisions, reminding us that

God's wisdom surpasses our own. It encourages resilience, sustaining our spirits when the moral path is fraught with difficulty.

Hope, on the other hand, invigorates our moral actions with a sense of purpose. It motivates us to engage in acts of kindness, justice, and mercy, knowing that each act contributes to the eventual realization of God's kingdom. In moments of moral uncertainty, hope anchors us, providing clarity and direction.

Love demands a radical empathy and compassion that transcends mere sentimentality. It challenges us to see the face of Christ in everyone, directing our actions towards the upliftment of others. In a world where division and strife are prevalent, acting in love is a powerful testimony to the reconciling work of the Gospel.

Integrating faith, hope, and love into our moral decision-making is a lifelong journey. It requires introspection, prayer, and a community of believers who support and challenge one another towards growth. No decision is too small to be informed by these virtues; from daily interactions to life-altering choices, they provide a compass that guides us towards ethical living.

The beauty of this moral framework lies in its universality and adaptability. Across cultures and contexts, the principles of faith, hope, and love offer a common language for ethical dialogue and discernment. They empower us to navigate the nuances of modern ethical challenges while anchored to timeless truths.

As we strive to be faithful witnesses of Christ in the world, the moral foundations of faith, hope, and love serve not only as guideposts but as beacons of light, illuminating the path towards a more just, compassionate, and loving world. By embodying these virtues, we participate in the redemptive work of God, crafting a narrative of hope and transformation in a world desperately in need of both.

The journey towards ethical maturity is marked by moments of profound insight and challenging reflection. Yet, through the lens of faith, hope, and love, we find not only guidance but empowerment. As we take each step, may we do so with the confidence that these virtues not only please God but also weave threads of grace into the fabric of our world.

In conclusion, the moral foundations of faith, hope, and love call us to a higher standard of living — one that mirrors the character of Christ. They challenge us to make decisions that reflect not only what is good but what is holy, urging us towards a life marked by grace, virtue, and unwavering commitment to the Gospel. As we navigate the complexities of the world, may these principles illuminate our path and shape our every action, bearing witness to the transformative power of living a life anchored in faith, propelled by hope, and guided by love.

Chapter 2:
The Authority of Scripture and
Tradition in Christian Ethics

In navigating the intricate terrain of Christian ethics, one cannot overlook the twin beacons of Scripture and Tradition, guiding believers through the undulating landscapes of moral decision-making. Chapter 2 embarks on a journey to understand how the Bible, as a divine compass, offers unparalleled wisdom and insight for ethical guidance, while Church Tradition, as the collective wisdom of the ages, enriches this guidance with lived experiences and interpretations passed down through generations. Scriptural authority is not merely about adhering to written texts; it's about engaging with them in a dynamic, living relationship that breathes life into daily decisions. Tradition, on the other hand, acts as a bridge, connecting the timeless truths of Scripture with the pressing questions of today's world. Together, they form a symbiotic partnership, each enhancing the understanding and application of the other. As we delve deeper into the significance of Scripture and Tradition, we embark on a transformative journey that not only informs our moral choices but also molds us into embodiments of Christ's love and wisdom in a world thirsty for integrity and compassion.

The Bible as a Source of Ethical Guidance

In the labyrinth of modern life, with its complex moral dilemmas and ethical quandaries, it's easy to feel lost. Yet, within the pages of the Bible, believers find a compass that offers direction, shedding light on the path of righteousness and guiding our steps in living a life that honors God. The Bible isn't just a collection of historical narratives, poetic verses, and prophetic utterances; it's a reservoir of wisdom, a guide for ethical living that speaks to every generation, including ours.

At the core of the Bible's message is love—love for God and love for one another. This dual commandment is the foundation upon which all other ethical teachings of the Bible rest. It's a simple yet profound statement that if heeded, can transform the way we navigate our daily decisions. In our interactions, whether in family, work, or society, applying this principle of love guides us towards actions that honor God and respect those around us.

But how do we decipher the specific ethical guidance the Bible offers for the myriad of decisions we face today, many of which seem so far removed from the world of the Bible? It begins with engaging the Scriptures not merely as a text to be studied but as a living word that speaks into our lives. Through prayerful reading and meditation on God's Word, we discover its relevance and application to our present context.

Moreover, understanding the Bible as a source of ethical guidance requires us to discern the underlying principles within its teachings. These principles transcend time and culture, providing a moral framework upon which we can build our ethical reasoning. For instance, the principle of justice, evidenced in the laws given to Israel and the prophets' cries against oppression, can inform our approach to social justice and advocacy today.

It's also vital to approach the Bible with humility, recognizing that our interpretation and understanding are not infallible. This humility opens the door to learning, to being corrected by the Spirit, and to growing in wisdom. It means we're open to dialoguing with others, engaging with church tradition, and considering the insights of theologians and scholars who have wrestled with ethical questions throughout Christian history.

Faith communities play a crucial role in this journey, providing a space to wrestle with ethical questions, to encourage one another in moral living, and to discern together how the Bible speaks into the specific challenges of our time. In these communities, we find accountability and support as we strive to align our lives more closely with biblical teachings.

One might wonder about the relevance of ancient ethics in a world vastly different from the one in which the Bible was written. Yet, the ethical challenges we face today are not as new as we might think. Issues of justice, integrity, love, and compassion are timeless. The Bible offers not only specific rules for conduct but also narratives that illustrate the complexity of moral decision-making and the consequences of our choices. Through these stories, we learn the importance of motive and intention, of mercy and humility, in ethical living.

Engaging with the Bible's ethical teachings also means grappling with texts that challenge our modern sensibilities. Not every instruction applies directly to our context. It requires discernment to understand which commands were culturally specific and which principles are eternal. It's a journey of faith, requiring trust in the Holy Spirit to guide us into all truth, as promised by Jesus.

Living ethically according to the Bible is not about legalism or following a set of rules to earn God's favor. It's about responding to God's grace with a life that reflects His love and righteousness. It's a journey marked by transformation, as the Holy Spirit shapes our desires, thoughts, and actions to mirror Christ's.

In pursuing biblical ethics, we're called to be agents of grace and light in a world marred by darkness and injustice. The ethical teachings of the Bible propel us into action, to care for the marginalized, to speak truth to power, and to embody the love of Christ in our communities. It's a high calling, one that demands our dedication and humility, but it's also a path filled with joy, peace, and the deep satisfaction that comes from living in alignment with God's will.

As we delve into the Scriptures, let us approach them with hearts open to transformation, minds ready to learn, and spirits willing to be guided. May the Bible serve not only as a source of ethical guidance but as a wellspring of hope, shaping us into beacons of God's love and righteousness in a world in desperate need of both.

So, let us cherish the Bible, immersing ourselves in its teachings, allowing it to critique our lives and inform our decisions. As we do, we'll find that its ancient wisdom speaks with startling relevance to the ethical decisions of our day, offering a roadmap for living that is as transformative as it is timeless.

Ultimately, the journey of ethical living according to the Bible is not one we undertake alone. It's a journey we share with the community of faith, past and present, guided by the Holy Spirit. It's a path marked by grace, where failure and forgiveness are part of the process, and where every step brings us closer to the heart of God. May we walk this path with courage, integrity, and an ever-deepening love for God and neighbor.

The Role of Church Tradition in Interpreting Ethical Norms

In navigating the vast seas of ethical questions, the church has long served as a lighthouse, guiding through the illumination of Scripture, complemented by the rich elegance of tradition. Tradition, in its essence, represents the collective wisdom and practices handed down through generations, offering a library of lived experiences underpinned by faith.

At first glance, the notion of tradition may appear as merely a relic of the past - static and unyielding. Yet, within the Christian context, tradition is dynamic, continually interacting with Scripture to shed light on the path of ethical decision-making. Its role is not to overshadow the biblical text but to serve as a lens through which its messages can be interpreted and understood in the context of contemporary dilemmas.

Church tradition is more than a mere accumulation of customs; it is a vibrant conversation stretching across centuries, involving saints, theologians, and believers. This dialogue provides continuity, ensuring that our ethical compasses are not solely determined by the zeitgeist but are anchored in a deeper, spiritual understanding that transcends time.

One might question how tradition can aid in interpreting ethical norms given the diversity and evolution of societal standards. The answer lies in the very bedrock of tradition - its ability to connect us with the foundational principles of faith, hope, and love, which guide Christian morality. Tradition serves not as a rigid rulebook but as a narrative that invites us to engage with ethical questions through the prism of these enduring virtues.

Within this framework, church tradition offers a repository of reflections on Scripture, providing insights into its application in various contexts. These reflections, derived from theological discussions, writings of the Church Fathers, and ecumenical councils, enrich our understanding and help articulate ethical norms that resonate with the challenges of the present.

Moreover, tradition nurtures community discernment, fostering an environment where believers can collectively ponder moral questions. It reminds us that we're part of a larger body, a communion of saints that stretches beyond the here and now. In this sense, the church acts as a moral compass, informed by both Scripture and the distilled wisdom of those who have walked the path of faith before us.

Yet, the relationship between Scripture and tradition is not without tension. There will always be debates and discussions about the correct interpretation and application of biblical principles. However, this tension is vital; it propels the church towards deeper understanding and more authentic ways of living out the teachings of Christ in a continually changing world.

Furthermore, tradition equips the church to grapple with new ethical questions that the early Christians could not have envisioned. Through the application of centuries-old wisdom to modern dilemmas, tradition provides a framework that helps maintain fidelity to Scriptural truths while engaging with the world in a relevant and meaningful way.

It is essential, however, to approach tradition with discernment, recognizing that not all practices or interpretations have equal weight or applicability to our current context. The Holy Spirit plays a crucial role in guiding the church through these complexities, ensuring that tradition serves to illuminate rather than obscure the core message of the Gospel.

Engaging with church tradition, therefore, demands humility and openness, an acknowledgment that we are part of a story much larger than ourselves. It calls us to listen attentively to the voices of the past, not as distant echoes but as participants in a dialogue that shapes how we live out our faith today.

In practical terms, incorporating tradition into ethical decision-making involves a conscious effort to study and reflect on the historical context of biblical teachings and how they have been applied throughout the centuries. It also means being active in community discernment processes, valuing the insights gained from collective reflection and prayer.

Ultimately, the role of church tradition in interpreting ethical norms is to bridge the gap between the timeless truths of Scripture and the evolving challenges of contemporary life. It ensures that our moral decision-making is both rooted in the faith and responsive to the world's needs—offering not just answers but wisdom for the journey.

As we continue to navigate the complexities of Christian ethics, let us embrace tradition with reverence and gratitude. Let us allow it to inform and enrich our understanding, guiding us toward living a life that reflects the fullness of the Gospel. For in the dance between Scripture and tradition, we find a rhythm that moves us closer to the heart of God, enabling us to act justly, love mercy, and walk humbly in a world yearning for hope.

In conclusion, the role of church tradition is indispensable in the quest for ethical living. It is a treasure trove of wisdom, waiting to be unlocked, offering guidance and light for the path ahead. As we move forward, may we do so with the confidence that we are accompanied by a cloud of witnesses, each step illuminated by the synergy of Scripture and the enduring legacy of tradition.

Chapter 3:
Virtue Ethics and the Christian Life

In traversing the path laid out in previous chapters, we've come to understand the scaffolding of Christian ethics, anchored deeply in scriptural wisdom and the rich tradition of the church. Our journey now ushers us into the heartland of virtue ethics and its relevance to living a Christian life. The essence of virtue ethics isn't just about adhering to a set of rules but involves cultivating a character that resonates with the likeness of Christ. It's about a transformation that emanates from within, a metamorphosis that aligns one's desires, actions, and habits with the kingdom values of justice, love, and humility.

Embracing virtue in our daily walk with God entails a radical reorientation of our lives. It's akin to planting seeds of divine qualities in the garden of our souls. Like any seed, these virtues need nurturing—through prayer, meditation on Scripture, and the sacraments—to bloom and flourish. Character is not built in a day but is the outcome of a lifelong pursuit of godliness, where our daily choices reflect the virtues we aspire to embody. In integrating these virtues into our daily lives, we are not merely aiming for moral excellence but are participating in God's redemptive work in the world, serving as beacons of light in a landscape often shadowed by moral ambiguity.

This chapter invites you on a quest to explore the intricate tapestry of virtues celebrated in the Christian tradition. Beyond abstract ideals, virtues are presented as practical pathways for navigating life's challenges, offering a compass for moral and spiritual growth. By weaving virtue ethics into the fabric of our lives, we're called to a higher purpose: living out the gospel in ways that touch lives, mend brokenness, and spread hope. It's here, in the everyday moments and decisions, that our character is tested and our commitment to Christ is exemplified. Through a life steeped in virtue, we testify to the transformative power of God's grace and the infinite possibilities of living in alignment with His will.

Exploring the Concept of Virtue in Christian Ethics

The journey into understanding Christian ethics leads us inevitably to the concept of virtue. Virtue, in its simplest form, is moral excellence. It's a disposition not only to act in ways that fulfill our intrinsic moral duties but to embody the good itself. Within the Christian tradition, this pursuit of virtue is not merely an exercise in self-improvement or moral philosophy; it's a response to a divine calling.

At the heart of Christian ethics is the belief that virtues are instilled and nurtured through our relationship with God. This divine relationship shapes our character, guiding us towards living a life that reflects the teachings of Jesus Christ. Virtues, therefore, are not just moral habits; they are expressions of our faith, hope, and love - the foundational stones of Christian morality.

Understanding virtue in the context of Christian ethics requires us to delve into Scripture, where virtues are often exemplified by the lives of biblical characters. The Beatitudes, for example, epitomize virtues that Christians are called to embody. Humility, mercy, righteousness, purity of heart - these are qualities that echo the call to live a life in communion with God and in service to others.

However, recognizing the virtues we are called to adopt is just the beginning. The real challenge, and indeed the journey of a lifetime, is integrating these virtues into the fabric of our daily lives. Every decision, interaction, and even moment of reflection becomes an opportunity to express virtue. But how does one begin such a task? Firstly, it involves a deep, personal connection with God through prayer, scripture, and communal worship. This spiritual grounding is essential for the cultivation of virtue.

Virtue also requires practice and perseverance. The virtues we admire in biblical characters or saints were not developed overnight but were the result of consistent effort and reliance on God's grace. Similarly, we must be patient with ourselves as we stumble, learn, and grow in virtue. The encouragement found in the company of fellow believers can be crucial in this endeavor, offering support, accountability, and understanding.

Moreover, the pursuit of virtue in Christian ethics is not limited to personal piety or moral self-improvement. It has a communal dimension that's pivotal. The virtues we cultivate within ourselves ought to ripple out into our families, communities, and beyond. Thus, a virtuous life is inherently relational, characterized by acts of kindness, justice, and love that reflect the very nature of God Himself.

This communal aspect of virtue brings to light another essential feature: discernment. In a world brimming with moral complexities, discerning the right course of action requires not only knowledge of the good but also the wisdom to apply it appropriately in varying circumstances. This wisdom, or practical virtue, is honed through the consistent practice of virtuous acts, guided by the Holy Spirit and informed by the teachings of the Church.

One must also grapple with the challenge of integrating virtues into a world often at odds with Christian values. In such a landscape, virtues like courage and faithfulness become crucial. They embolden

Christians to stand firm in their convictions, offering hope and light in the face of societal pressures and moral relativism.

The transformation into a virtuous person is ultimately a journey towards becoming more like Christ. It's an ongoing process of sanctification, where each act of virtue draws us closer to the person God created us to be. This transformative process is not solitary but is supported by the grace of God, the teachings of Scripture, and the fellowship of the Church.

In contemplating the role of virtue in Christian ethics, one is reminded of Paul's letters to the Galatians, where he lists the fruits of the Spirit: love, joy, peace, patience, kindness, goodness, faithfulness, gentleness, and self-control. These virtues encapsulate the Christian ethical life, serving as tangible expressions of our faith and beacons of God's presence in the world.

Indeed, virtues are both the gifts and the tasks given to us. They are gifts in that they are graced capacities bestowed by God, enabling us to live in a way that reflects His nature. Yet, they are also tasks, demanding our active participation and cooperation with God's grace.

As we navigate the nuanced and often challenging pathways of life, the pursuit of virtue provides a compass. It offers direction in moments of moral ambiguity and strength when faced with difficult choices. More than mere moral guidelines, virtues are the very essence of our Christian identity, calling us to live lives of holiness and love.

In closing, the exploration of virtue in Christian ethics is not merely an academic exercise but a call to action. It's an invitation to embark on a transformative journey, one that shapes us into individuals who not only understand the good but who are committed to embodying it in every aspect of our lives. In doing so, we not only find our true selves but also become conduits of God's grace, lighting the way for others in a world that yearns for hope and redemption.

Thus, the call to virtue is a profound one, challenging us to look beyond our immediate desires and to embrace a higher calling. It beckons us to a life of service, humility, and love, echoing the life of Christ Himself. In embracing this call, we find that the pursuit of virtue is not a burden, but rather a path to true freedom and fulfillment.

Integrating Virtue into Daily Life

In the bustling flow of everyday life, where pressures mount and distractions abound, integrating virtue into daily life emerges as a beacon of guidance for Christians striving to live in alignment with their faith. The transition from understanding virtue in theory to embodying it in the practical moments of our day is a journey that touches the core of our existence.

At the heart of Christian ethics is the call to embody virtues - those inner qualities that reflect the character of Christ. Love, patience, kindness, humility, and self-control are not just ideals to admire from afar; they are attainable traits to weave into the fabric of our daily routines. This transformation begins with a conscious decision to make these virtues the lens through which we view and engage with the world around us.

One of the first steps in this journey is to cultivate a daily habit of reflection. In the quiet moments of the morning or the stillness of the evening, take time to reflect on the virtues you wish to see flourish in your life. Ask yourself, "How did I embody these virtues today?" or "Where was I challenged?" This practice of self-examination opens a pathway for growth and deepens our understanding and application of Christian ethics in our lives.

Prayer is another vital component in integrating virtue. Through prayer, we seek guidance from God, drawing strength and wisdom beyond our own. Prayer positions our hearts to receive the grace needed to transform our character and actions. It is in the silence of sincere prayer that we often find the clarity and conviction to live out our virtues amidst life's complexities.

Scripture offers a rich reservoir of wisdom on how to live a virtuous life. Regular engagement with the Word of God not only educates us on what virtue looks like but also inspires us to implement it. Stories of faith, sacrifice, and redemption within the Bible serve as powerful examples of virtue in action. Let these narratives challenge and change you, molding you more into the likeness of Christ.

Community plays a crucial role in our virtuous journey. Surround yourself with individuals who uplift and encourage your pursuit of a virtuous life. The Christian community offers support, accountability, and the shared wisdom of those who walk alongside you in faith. It's in these relationships that virtues are both tested and strengthened, creating a living workshop of virtue in action.

Service is the outward expression of inward virtue. Look for opportunities to serve within your church, local community, or beyond. Acts of service, big or small, become the canvas on which your virtues paint the beauty of Christ's love to the world. It's through service that we practice humility, generosity, and compassion, bringing the essence of Christian ethics to life.

Patience is essential on this journey. The integration of virtue into daily life is a process, marked by progress and setbacks. Treat yourself with the same grace God extends to you. Embrace failures as opportunities to learn and grow, not as final verdicts on your character.

In moments of decision, let virtue guide your choices. When faced with moral dilemmas or everyday decisions, ask yourself, "Which option best reflects the virtues I am committed to embodying?" This approach anchors your actions in integrity and aligns your decisions with your deepest values.

Remember, the goal of integrating virtue is not perfection but faithfulness. Walking in virtue is a dynamic journey of becoming more like Christ, one step at a time. With each step, we contribute to a larger narrative of hope and transformation, both in ourselves and in the world around us.

Maintain a posture of learning. Stay open to the lessons life presents, and be willing to adjust your approach as you grow in understanding. The pursuit of virtue is a lifetime endeavor, enriched by each new insight and experience.

Finally, celebrate the victories, no matter how small. Acknowledge moments when you see the fruits of your efforts to live virtuously. Share these victories with your community as a testament to God's active work in your life. These celebrations nurture a spirit of gratitude and encourage perseverance on the virtuous path.

Integrating virtue into daily life is more than a noble pursuit; it is a practical expression of our faith. In doing so, we become beacons of light in a world in desperate need of the hope and love that flow from a life aligned with the heart of God. Let us commit to this journey with determination, guided by grace and empowered by the Spirit, to reflect the beauty of Christ in all we do.

As we navigate the complexities of life, may our commitment to living out our virtues with intention and purpose be our guide. The path may not always be easy, but the destination—a life marked by the love and grace of Christ—is worth every step. Let virtue be the compass that steers us, the anchor that holds us, and the light that leads us home.

Chapter 4:
Decision-Making and the Will of God

In the intricate journey of life, where each step molds our destiny, "Decision-Making and the Will of God" stands as a beacon of divine guidance, inviting us to delve deeply into the relationship between our daily choices and the divine blueprint. At the heart of Christian living lies the profound challenge of discerning God's will in the myriad decisions we face. This chapter unfolds a tapestry of spiritual wisdom, interweaving biblical insights with practical steps to align our choices with God's intentions. It's not merely about choosing the path of least resistance; rather, it's an endeavor to listen, with a heart tuned to God's whispers, deciphering His will amid life's clamor. Whether it's choosing a career path, nurturing relationships, or facing ethical dilemmas, understanding God's will becomes a journey of trust and transformation. By integrating prayer, Scripture, and the counsel of the faithful, we embark on a quest not just to make decisions, but to form a deeper communion with the Divine, learning to discern not only in moments of solitude but also in the midst of community. This chapter doesn't promise easy answers but offers a compass by which to navigate the complexities of life, making each decision a stepping stone towards fulfilling our God-given purpose.

Determining God's Will in Difficult Decisions

In our journey through the narrow path of life, the question of aligning our decisions with God's will emerges as a profound challenge.

The complexity of modern life introduces difficult decisions at every turn, leaving many to wonder how they can discern God's direction when faced with choices that the Scriptures do not directly address.

The process of determining God's will in difficult decisions begins with seeking a heart attuned to the spiritual realm. This involves a deliberate effort to cultivate a relationship with God, where prayer and meditation are not just practices but lifelines that connect us to the divine wisdom that guides our steps.

Scripture, while it may not possess a verse that explicitly spells out the answer to every quandary we face, provides principles that serve as our moral compass. The Psalms and Proverbs, in particular, are rich with advice on seeking wisdom, understanding, and guidance from God. Aligning our choices with the truths found in these sacred texts is a fundamental step in discerning God's will.

Moreover, the role of the Holy Spirit cannot be understated. As believers, we are given the gift of the Holy Spirit, whose role is to guide, convict, and enlighten us. Listening for the still, small voice requires intentionality and patience, but it is crucial for those seeking to make decisions that honor God.

Another pivotal aspect is the counsel of godly mentors and friends. God often speaks through the wisdom of those who have walked the faith longer than we have. Their perspectives, grounded in years of following God, can shed light on our paths, providing clarity amid confusion. "As iron sharpens iron, so one person sharpens another" (Proverbs 27:17), illustrates the value of godly counsel in making sound decisions.

Additionally, it's vital to recognize that God's will does not always equate to the easiest path. On the contrary, the decisions that align with God's purpose often require sacrifice, discomfort, and faith that steps out into the unknown. It's in the challenging decisions that our faith is both tested and strengthened.

In this quest for divine guidance, one must also embrace a posture of humility and surrender. Acknowledging that our understanding is limited and submitting our desires to God's will are key elements in discerning the right course of action. This surrender, though it may seem daunting, brings peace and assurance that our decisions are rooted in a desire to honor God.

Openness to redirection plays a significant role in this discernment process. Sometimes, despite our best efforts to seek God's will, we find that the doors we hoped would open are closed, and paths we thought were right lead to nowhere. It is in these moments we must trust that God is redirecting us toward His perfect will, even when it's beyond our understanding.

Throughout this process, it's imperative to remember that seeking God's will is not a one-time event but a continual pursuit. Decisions, both big and small, present opportunities to trust and follow God more closely. Each choice, when laid before God in a pursuit of His will, strengthens our faith and molds us more into the likeness of Christ.

Moreover, the peace of God, which transcends all understanding, is promised to guard our hearts and minds in Christ Jesus (Philippians 4:7). This peace is a signpost, indicating when we've made decisions in alignment with God's will. It is a divine calm that persists even when circumstances remain uncertain or difficult.

In addition to inner peace, observable outcomes can also guide us. While we do not judge God's will solely based on outcomes, seeing how choices lead to fruitfulness in God's kingdom or contribute to our spiritual growth can affirm the direction we've chosen. These outcomes, however, may not be immediate and require a perspective that looks beyond the present moment.

It's also crucial to address the fear of missing God's will. This fear can paralyze and lead to indecision. Understanding that God's grace covers our mistakes and that He can work through all circumstances is freeing. Even when we make wrong turns, our loving Father is able to reroute us back to His plans.

Finally, it is important to act. Faith without action is lifeless. Once we have sought God's guidance through prayer, Scripture, counsel, and introspection, we must take steps forward. Indecision can sometimes be a greater error than an incorrect decision, as it stalls our spiritual progress and development.

In conclusion, determining God's will in difficult decisions is a multifaceted journey that involves intimate communication with God, wisdom from Scripture and godly counsel, and the courage to step out in faith. Though fraught with challenges, it is a journey that ultimately deepens our faith, enriching our walk with God.

As we navigate life's complexities, let us hold fast to the promise that God is with us, guiding each step. By seeking His will above all, we can navigate even the most perplexing decisions with confidence and peace, assured that we are never alone in the journey.

Practical Steps for Discerning God's Direction

In our journey through life, navigating the waters of decision-making can feel overwhelming, especially when we're striving to align our choices with God's will. The divine compass we seek is not always as clear as we'd like, but with intentional practice and spiritual discipline, we can hone our ability to discern God's direction. This process is not about seeking signs in every corner but about cultivating a relationship with God that illuminates our path.

First and foremost, prayer is the bedrock of discernment. It's not merely about presenting our desires or seeking confirmation for our plans but engaging in an open dialogue with God. Through prayer, we create the space for God to speak into our lives, to shape our desires, and to guide our steps. The key is consistency and honesty in our prayer life, approaching God with an open heart ready to listen.

Scripture provides a solid foundation for understanding God's character and His will for humanity. Regularly immersing ourselves in the word of God equips us with the wisdom to make decisions that align with biblical principles. When faced with a decision, seek out passages that speak to the situation or the underlying moral principles. Meditating on these scriptures can offer clarity and peace in the decision-making process.

Another vital step is seeking godly counsel. Surrounding ourselves with individuals who walk closely with God and embody wisdom can provide invaluable insight. These mentors can offer a perspective that is both challenging and affirming, grounded in a deep understanding of God's ways. However, discernment is required to ensure that the advice aligns with scripture and the promptings of the Holy Spirit.

Engaging in a period of fasting can be a powerful tool for discernment. By setting aside physical nourishment, we signal a deep dependence on God and open ourselves up to His guidance in a unique way. Fasting, combined with prayer and meditation on scripture, can sharpen our spiritual sensitivity and clear the clutter of our minds and hearts.

The Holy Spirit plays a crucial role in discerning God's direction. As believers, we are equipped with this indwelling presence, a helper who guides us into all truth. Cultivating a sensitivity to the Holy Spirit's promptings requires a surrendered heart and a willingness to obey, even when it leads us out of our comfort zones. Regular times of quiet and solitude can help us tune in to the Spirit's whisperings.

Being part of a faith community offers support and accountability as we seek to discern and follow God's will. The shared wisdom, diverse perspectives, and collective prayer found within a community can confirm or challenge our sense of direction. Moreover, observing the ways God is at work in the lives of others can inspire and guide us in our own journey.

Keeping a journal of prayers, insights from scripture, words of counsel, and personal reflections is a practical way to track God's movement in our lives. Often, writing down our thoughts and prayers can bring clarity to our confusion and reveal patterns or confirmations we might not have noticed otherwise.

Staying attentive to circumstances is also essential. While circumstances alone should not dictate our decisions, they can serve as indicators when considered alongside scripture, prayer, counsel, and the Holy Spirit's guidance. Sometimes, God opens or closes doors as a way of leading us in a particular direction.

Patience is crucial in discernment. We often desire immediate answers, but God's timing is perfect, and waiting on Him can be an act of faith and trust. During periods of waiting, continue to engage deeply with God through prayer, scripture, and community. Trust that He is at work, shaping our character and preparing us for what is to come.

Acting in faith is the culmination of discernment. Once we feel a sense of direction from God, we're called to step out in faith, even when the outcome is uncertain. Faith is the assurance of things hoped for, the conviction of things not seen. Taking action based on our discernment demonstrates our trust in God and our willingness to be used by Him.

Reflecting on past decisions and discerning moments can provide encouragement and wisdom for current decisions. Looking back at how God has guided and provided in the past can bolster our faith and trust in His continued faithfulness.

While seeking God's direction, we must also be prepared to accept His answer, whether it's a 'yes,' 'no,' or 'wait.' Surrendering our desires to God's will is an ongoing process, one that requires humility and trust. Remember, His ways are higher than our ways, and His thoughts higher than our thoughts.

Cultivating a lifestyle of worship, where every aspect of our lives is an offering to God, aligns our hearts with His. Living in worship allows us to view our decisions not simply as choices we make but as expressions of our love and devotion to God. This perspective can transform our approach to decision-making, grounding it in our relationship with the Divine.

In conclusion, discerning God's direction is a journey of deepening relationship with Him, grounded in prayer, scripture, and community. It's a process marked by trust, obedience, and a commitment to walking in the way of Jesus. Remember, God is more interested in who we are becoming than in what we are doing. As we seek His direction, let it be an opportunity to grow in faith, character, and love.

Chapter 5:
The Sanctity of Human Life

Moving seamlessly from understanding God's will in our decisions, we're drawn into a profound reverence for life itself, encapsulated in the sacred belief in its sanctity. This chapter dives deep into the heartbeat of Christian ethics, exalting the inherent value of every human life as a reflection of divine craftsmanship. The significance of viewing life through this lens can't be overstated—it transforms our interactions, informs our choices, and illuminates the path to embodying Christ's compassion in a world yearning for empathy and understanding. Here, we don't merely explore the biblical perspective on the value of life; we're invited into a journey that considers the challenging ethical terrains of abortion and euthanasia with sensitivity, grace, and a steadfast commitment to preserving the dignity bestowed upon each person by their Creator. The conversation here is not about dictating rights and wrongs but about equipping ourselves with a Christ-centered framework that enables us to navigate life's most challenging moral dilemmas with wisdom, love, and an unwavering respect for the sanctity of human life. Embracing this vision propels us beyond mere intellectual assent, inspiring us to become beacons of light and hope, in a society grappling with complex ethical issues, illuminating the ineffable worth of every individual.

A Biblical Perspective on the Value of Life

In the corridors of history and the quiet corners of our hearts, the question of life's intrinsic value whispers persistently. The Christian narrative, deeply embedded in the tapestry of Scripture, offers profound insights into this question. From the Genesis account of creation to the redemptive climax of the cross, the Bible articulates a resounding affirmation of the sanctity of human life.

At the outset, the creation narrative sets a foundation for understanding life's value. "So God created mankind in his own image, in the image of God he created them; male and female he created them" (Genesis 1:27). This divine imprint bestows upon human life an immeasurable worth, distinguishing humanity in the vast expanse of creation. It's a declaration that every breath, every heartbeat, is imbued with significance because it reflects the Creator himself.

The psalmist, in a moment of contemplation, marvels at this reality, saying, "I praise you because I am fearfully and wonderfully made; your works are wonderful, I know that full well" (Psalm 139:14). There's a recognition here that life is not a random occurrence but a masterpiece crafted by the divine Artist, each detail known and each moment ordained.

Yet, the biblical narrative also confronts us with the reality of a world scarred by sin. The sacredness of life is violated through acts like Cain's violence against Abel, illustrating the deep fracture sin introduces into the human story. Still, even amidst humanity's failings, God's commitment to life's sanctity remains unwavering. The biblical laws, often seen as stringent, consistently seek to protect the vulnerable, embodying a divine concern for all aspects of life.

In the unfolding story of redemption, the prophets dream of a restored creation where the lion and the lamb coexist peacefully, symbolizing a renewal of life's sanctity in a reconciled world. This vision reaches its fulfillment in Jesus, whose ministry consistently affirms life's worth. Jesus heals the sick, welcomes the marginalized, and cherishes the overlooked, demonstrating that the value of life transcends societal labels and conditions.

The pinnacle of the biblical affirmation of life's value is found in the narrative of the cross and resurrection. In the act of laying down His own life, Jesus provides the ultimate testament to the value God places on human life. It's a declaration that life is worth redeeming, worth restoring, and worth sacrificing everything for. And in the resurrection, we see the guarantee of this promise—a foretaste of the day when every tear will be wiped away, and life will flourish in its full glory.

Faced with this rich biblical tapestry, the Christian response to life's sanctity is multifaceted. It calls for a deep reverence for life, recognizing that each person is a bearer of God's image. It challenges us to be agents of healing, embodying Jesus' restorative work in our interactions and societies. And it inspires hope, anchoring us in the promise of a restored creation where life's intrinsic value is fully realized.

In practical terms, this means advocating for the protection of life at all stages, from the womb to the final breath. It involves opposing injustices that degrade human dignity, whether through poverty, racism, or violence. And it entails caring for creation, understanding that the stewardship of the earth is intrinsically linked to the respect of life God has entrusted us with.

Moreover, the biblical perspective on life's value informs our approach to complex ethical issues, from bioethics to the treatment of the elderly and the terminally ill. In every question, the sanctity of life serves as a guiding principle, urging us toward decisions that honor the image of God in every individual.

This view of life also profoundly shapes the Christian community's identity. In a world where life is often measured by utility, efficiency, or convenience, the church stands as a counter-culture that celebrates life as a sacred gift. It's a community where every individual, regardless of their utility or status, is valued and loved—a reflection of the divine love that cherishes each person unconditionally.

In embracing this biblical perspective, Christians are called to a life of radical love and sacrificial service. It's a path that mirrors Jesus' own, marked by compassion, generosity, and a relentless affirmation of life's worth. As we walk this path, we embody the hope of the Gospel—a hope that affirms, against all odds, that life is sacred, precious, and worthy of our utmost reverence and care.

As we reflect on the biblical perspective on the value of life, we stand at the intersection of divine promise and human responsibility. It's a calling to behold the sanctity of life through the lens of Scripture and to act in ways that reflect this profound truth. In a world yearning for hope and healing, this perspective offers light, guiding us toward a future where the fullness of life is celebrated for the divine gift that it is.

Thus, the sanctity of human life, as illumined by the Bible, is not merely an abstract doctrine but a living, breathing truth that shapes how we view ourselves, others, and the world around us. It challenges us to look beyond the surface, recognizing the divine spark within each person and honoring it in our thoughts, words, and actions. As we journey through the complexities of life, may this truth anchor us, guide us, and inspire us to be beacons of life-affirming love in a world in desperate need of it.

Ethical Considerations in Abortion and Euthanasia

Within the mosaic of Christian ethics, the sanctity of human life shines as a fundamental principle, guiding us through the murky waters of moral dilemmas. As we delve into the ethical considerations surrounding abortion and euthanasia, it's essential to anchor our reflections in the bedrock of this principle. Both issues, deeply divisive and emotionally charged, challenge us to weigh the value of life through the lens of compassion, justice, and divine wisdom.

Abortion, a topic that stirs deep emotions and varying opinions even among Christians, requires us to ask fundamental questions. What does it mean to value life? At what point does life begin? Scripture, while not addressing abortion directly, affirms life as a sacred gift, weaving a narrative of life's intrinsic worth from conception to natural death. From the poetic declarations of being knit together in the womb in Psalms to the prophetic callings assigned before birth in Jeremiah, the Bible underscores God's intimate involvement in the creation of each life.

Thus, approaching the issue of abortion demands a heartfelt engagement with these scriptural affirmations, alongside a compassionate understanding of the complex realities faced by those considering abortion. It's not merely a legal debate but a profound ethical quandary that beckons Christians to offer love, support, and viable alternatives to women in distressing circumstances, embodying Christ's love in action.

Euthanasia, or the act of intentionally ending a life to relieve pain and suffering, presents a challenge of a different nature. Here, the question pivots from the commencement of life to its conclusion. In societies where autonomy and individual rights are paramount, euthanasia is increasingly viewed as a compassionate choice. Yet, the Christian perspective insists on the intrinsic value of every moment of life, including its final stages.

Belief in the sanctity of human life compels us to consider alternatives that honor the dignity of the dying, promoting palliative care and emotional support for those nearing life's end. It's a call to see Christ in the face of the suffering and to be His hands and feet in providing comfort, not hastening death.

These issues also raise crucial questions about human autonomy and divine sovereignty. The temptation to play God, to assume full control over life and death, confronts us with the profound Christian truth that life, in all its stages and forms, is a stewardship, not an ownership. We are called to trust in God's encompassing love and wisdom, even when faced with the most challenging decisions.

In navigating these ethical minefields, the Christian community must engage in open, honest conversations, embracing both the complexity of the issues and the diversity of thought within the faith. These discussions should be marked by grace, empathy, and a shared commitment to uphold the value of life as a reflection of our Creator's image.

Moreover, the church's response to abortion and euthanasia should extend beyond ideological debates, manifesting in practical expressions of love and support. From providing resources for expectant mothers to offering compassionate care for the terminally ill, Christians are called to be active proponents of life in all its phases.

To those wrestling with decisions about abortion or euthanasia, the Christian message is one of hope and redemption. It speaks to the power of grace to heal and restore, offering a vision of life's sanctity that endures even in the face of pain, despair, and moral ambiguity. This message does not minimize the gravity of these choices but offers a path forward grounded in love, forgiveness, and the relentless belief in the possibility of new beginnings.

Indeed, ethical considerations in abortion and euthanasia deeply challenge us, but they also offer opportunities for profound spiritual growth. Through prayerful reflection and engagement with these issues, we can deepen our understanding of what it means to cherish and protect life as followers of Christ.

As we continue this journey, let us be guided by humility, seeking wisdom through the Holy Spirit. Our discussions and actions regarding the sanctity of life should reflect the compassion, grace, and love that Jesus demonstrated throughout His ministry. In doing so, we not only navigate ethical dilemmas with integrity but also bear witness to the transformative power of the Gospel in addressing the most complex challenges of our time.

In conclusion, the ethical considerations surrounding abortion and euthanasia invite us into a deeper exploration of the sanctity of human life. Anchored in a biblical worldview, our approach to these issues should be characterized by compassion, love, and a steadfast commitment to uphold the value of every life. As we engage with these challenges, may our hearts be open to the guiding presence of God, leading us to walk in truth, grace, and relentless hope.

Chapter 6:
Marriage, Family, and Sexual Ethics

In navigating the sacred terrains of marriage, family, and sexual ethics, we're invited into a profound exploration of love, commitment, and integrity through a Christian lens. This chapter serves as a beacon, illuminating the path for those seeking to understand these aspects of life not just as societal constructs but as divine opportunities to embody the virtues of faithfulness, patience, and selflessness. In the context of marriage, we delve deep into the covenantal relationship that mirrors Christ's unwavering commitment to the Church, emphasizing the spiritual and moral foundations that fortify this union. Our discourse extends into family life, where the nurturing of children and the cultivation of godly values knit the very fabric of a Christ-centered home. Sexual ethics, often shrouded in controversy and confusion, are approached with grace and truth, unraveling the gift of sexuality as intended by God, and the call to honor it within the bounds of marriage. As we confront the modern challenges that cloud these institutions—be it through societal shifts, technological advances, or cultural relativism—we anchor our understanding in the timeless truths of Scripture, guided by wisdom and a heart open to God's direction. This chapter isn't merely a set of rules or a moralistic guide but an invitation to journey through life's relational aspects with a compass aligned to Christ's teachings, ensuring our footsteps lead not only to fulfilling relationships but to a deeper communion with the divine.

Christian Views on Marriage and Sexual Integrity

Within the Christian tradition, marriage is revered as a sacred covenant, a mutual partnership designed not only for the companionship and mutual support of both partners but also as a profound symbol of Christ's relationship with the Church. This deep-rooted perspective steers the Christian understanding of both marriage and sexual integrity, framing them within the boundaries of faithfulness, commitment, and respect.

The essence of sexual integrity in Christianity transcends merely avoiding certain actions or behaviors. It embodies the cultivation of virtue, the commitment to fidelity, and the pursuit of purity of heart. This pursuit is not a burdensome imposition but a joyful response to God's love and a desire to mirror that love in all relationships, especially within the context of marriage.

Scripture, particularly within the New Testament, provides guiding principles on these matters. It speaks to the sanctity of the marriage bed, the importance of fidelity, and the value of self-control. These scriptural teachings are not outdated edicts; instead, they offer timeless wisdom on how to foster deep, meaningful connections based on mutual respect and love.

Moreover, the Christian view on sexual integrity challenges the modern, often commodified view of sexuality, proposing a radical alternative that prioritizes the dignity of every individual. In a world where relationships can be subject to the sway of convenience and desire, the Christian ethic stands as a beacon, advocating for enduring commitments that reflect the steadfast love of God.

Understanding marriage as a divine vocation also shapes the Christian approach to this sacred union. Marriage isn't just a social contract but a calling that involves nurturing, growth, and, at times, sacrifice. This vocation is premised on the belief that through their union, both partners are sanctified, drawing closer to God and each other in their journey through life.

The challenge of living out these principles in the current age cannot be understated. In a culture that often celebrates personal fulfillment at the expense of communal well-being, the Christian ethic of marriage and sexual integrity calls for a counter-cultural stance. It promotes a vision of love that is self-giving, other-centered, and deeply rooted in faith.

This vision extends to the understanding of family life as well. The Christian household is envisaged as a place where virtues are nurtured, faith is lived out boldly, and the dignity of every member is upheld. Sexual integrity, within this framework, is about more than personal purity; it's about creating an environment where every person can thrive.

At times, the path to maintaining sexual integrity and a holy marriage may seem daunting. The pressures and temptations of the world are real, and the journey is not without its challenges. However, the Christian tradition offers not just rules to follow but a community of faith for support, practices for spiritual growth, and, most importantly, the grace of God to renew and sustain.

Prayer, both personal and communal, is a fundamental resource on this journey. Through prayer, individuals and couples draw closer to God, seeking wisdom, strength, and guidance. The sacramental life of the Church also provides means of grace, equipping believers to live out their callings with integrity and love.

It's essential to approach discussions about marriage and sexual integrity with a spirit of humility and compassion. The Christian community is called to be a place of healing, not judgment; offering support to those who struggle while upholding a high standard of moral conduct. This delicate balance is achieved not through our own strength, but through reliance on the transformative power of grace.

For those navigating difficulties in marriage or striving to live lives of purity, the testimonies of countless believers who have walked this path before can offer encouragement and hope. The saints, in their diverse experiences, demonstrate that though the journey is challenging, it is also marked by profound joy and fulfillment.

In conclusion, the Christian views on marriage and sexual integrity provide a rich, profoundly counter-cultural perspective that offers a way toward true fulfillment and joy in relationships. This path isn't marked by an easy, one-size-fits-all solution but by a journey of ongoing conversion, growth, and deepening love. As believers navigate the complexities of modern life, the timeless truths of the Christian faith serve as both anchor and compass, guiding towards a horizon of hope and redemption.

Let us, then, embrace this call with courage and faith, trusting in the God who is love to lead us through every challenge and joy. In our marriages, our families, and our personal lives, may we reflect the beauty of a love that is pure, selfless, and truly Christ-like. The journey towards sexual integrity and a holy marriage is, indeed, a pathway to experiencing the fullness of life that God desires for each of His children.

Navigating Modern Challenges in Family Life

In our journey through the landscape of Christian ethics, we encounter the vibrant tapestry of family life, woven with threads of tradition and contemporary fibers. This confluence presents an array of modern challenges, each demanding our attention and discernment. The essence of navigating these challenges lies not merely in adherence to directives but in embodying the principles of faith, hope, and love within the familial context.

Modern family life often finds itself at the crossroads of technological advancement and traditional values. The digital era, while offering unprecedented connectivity, also introduces complexities that test the bounds of privacy, intimacy, and communication within the familial unit. It's here, in the glow of screens and the buzz of notifications, that we must rekindle the virtue of presence—being fully with one another, undistracted and engaged.

The structure of families has evolved, with diversity in configurations now more prevalent. Single-parent families, blended families, and those with same-sex parents seek acknowledgment and love within their communities. Our challenge is to extend the hand of fellowship, understanding that love does not discriminate, and neither should our compassion and support for all of God's children.

Discussions on sexual ethics, once perhaps more straightforward, have burgeoned into dialogues rich with questions about identity, orientation, and expression. Here, we find a field ripe for empathy and understanding, guided by the unwavering belief that everyone is made in the image of God. The task at hand is to engage in these discussions with grace, aiming not to judge but to understand and uphold the dignity of every person.

The rhythm of family life has also changed, with both parents often engaged in careers outside the home. This shift necessitates a rebalancing of responsibilities and a reimagining of roles, breaking free from traditional molds to embrace a partnership model in upbringing and household duties. It's an invitation to practice servitude and humility, honoring each other's contributions as equally valuable.

Amid the hustle of modern life, the sanctity of mealtime as a family gathering point has waned. Reviving this tradition is not about the act of eating but about reclaiming a sacred space for connection, conversation, and communion with each other and with God. It is around the table that we share our daily bread and our lives, weaving stories that bind us together.

The intrusion of work and external commitments into family time has blurred boundaries, often leaving families fragmented and individuals isolated. Setting aside intentional time for family, free from the intrusion of work emails or school assignments, is a radical act of prioritizing relationships over productivity. It's a statement that, in our hearts, we serve our families with the same dedication we give to our professions.

Consumer culture and the pursuit of material wealth pose subtle threats to the fabric of family life, tempting us with the illusion that happiness can be purchased. In resistance, we're called to foster contentment and simplicity, finding joy not in possessions but in the richness of our relationships and the blessings of everyday moments shared with loved ones.

The challenge of nurturing faith within the family amidst a secular society stands tall. It beckons us to be beacons of light, cultivating practices of prayer, worship, and biblical study as a family. These practices anchor us in a shared faith journey, inviting God into the heart of our home, guiding us through the complexities of life with His wisdom and grace.

As families navigate the landscapes of loss and change, whether through bereavement, separation, or other life transitions, the Christian community is called to be a source of comfort and support. In these valleys, we are reminded of the power of communal prayer, the ministry of presence, and the healing that comes from walking alongside each other in times of sorrow and uncertainty.

The concept of discipline within the family, too, calls for a measured and loving approach. In a world quick to criticize, our call is to correct with love, guiding our children towards righteousness not with fear, but with an understanding hand and a listening heart. It is through our actions that we teach the values of respect, integrity, and compassion.

In addressing these modern challenges, it's critical to approach family life as a dynamic and evolving journey. It's a journey that calls for adaptability, forgiveness, and an ongoing commitment to growth, both individually and collectively. We lean into the promise that where love and respect are sown, joy and harmony will surely grow.

Let us remember that navigating the complexities of modern family life is not a task we undertake alone but in partnership with the Divine. Through prayer, reflection, and the wisdom of Scripture, we find the strength and guidance to face each new day with hope and love.

As we move forward, let our families be places of sanctuary and light, where every member feels valued, understood, and deeply loved. May our homes reflect the love of Christ, radiating warmth and welcome, and may we embrace the challenges of our time with courage, faith, and a steadfast commitment to embodying Christian virtues in all aspects of our family life.

In closing, let us take to heart the call to navigate the modern challenges in family life not as burdens but as opportunities to deepen our faith, strengthen our bonds, and testify to the transformative power of God's love in the world. With grace as our guide, we journey together, hand in hand, toward a future bright with promise for all families.

Chapter 7:
Work, Wealth, and Stewardship

In the pursuit of living a life that resonates with Christian values, understanding the ethical implications of work, wealth, and stewardship becomes indispensable. Work is not merely a means to an end but is fundamentally a vocation through which we honor God, reflecting the creative workmanship of our Creator. The dignity of labor, regardless of its nature, calls us to approach our occupations with integrity and purpose, recognizing the opportunity to contribute positively to society and the kingdom of God. Meanwhile, wealth, often misconstrued as an indicator of God's favor, demands a profound reevaluation. The true measurement of wealth in the Christian life is not found in the abundance of possessions but in the depth of generosity and the willingness to serve and uplift the less fortunate. This chapter delves into the heart of stewardship, challenging us to steward our resources, time, and the environment with wisdom and discernment. It's here that we're reminded that everything we own is not ours but is entrusted to us by God, calling us to manage it with the mindfulness of His kingdom's values. Embracing this trilateral relationship between our work, wealth, and stewardship paves the way for a life that is not only fulfilling but also glorifying to God, inviting us to participate in a larger story of redemption and restoration.

The Ethical Dimension of Work

In the heart of living a life that mirrors the grace and love that's been given to us, understanding the ethical dimension of work is critical. Within the broad narrative of our lives, the work we do isn't just a way to earn living but is a core part of our identity and our service to the world around us. This ethos is deeply rooted in the Christian tradition, which teaches that our labor is not only a participation in God's ongoing creation but also a form of worship.

At the cornerstone of the Christian ethic of work is the concept of stewardship. This perspective urges us to view our skills, opportunities, and indeed, our very call to work, as gifts entrusted to us by God. In this light, our work becomes more than a personal endeavor—it transforms into a mission, a divine assignment to influence the world positively, and nurture the creation that God so lovingly crafted.

The principle of stewardship challenges us to reflect on the nature and outcome of our work critically. It prompts a serious evaluation: Does our work contribute to the betterment of society? Does it align with the principles of justice, mercy, and compassion that are so central to the Christian faith? These questions are fundamental in navigating the complex waters of our modern work environments, where the drive for success often overshadows the more profound call to serve.

Moreover, the ethical dimension of work also encompasses the manner in which we conduct ourselves within our professional environments. The virtues of honesty, integrity, and diligence are not just personal values, but are testimonies of our faith in action. They speak volumes about who we are and the God we serve, serving as a light in places that can often be shadowed by competition and self-centered ambition.

However, embracing the ethical dimension of work is not without its challenges. In a world glorified by the idol of success, ethical considerations can sometimes seem like a roadblock to advancement or achievement. Here, the story of Daniel in the Bible offers profound guidance. Despite facing intense pressure and threats to his life, Daniel remained unwavering in his integrity and his commitment to God. His story is a powerful reminder that our ultimate accountability is not to our bosses or clients, but to God.

Additionally, the ethical dimension of work compels us to address issues of fairness and equality in the workplace. The Christian ethic teaches us that every human being is created in the image of God and thereby deserves to be treated with dignity and respect. This belief lays the foundation for advocating for fair wages, safe working conditions, and equal opportunities for all employees.

In the same vein, the ethic of love challenges us to view our coworkers not as competitors or tools for personal gain but as neighbors and fellow children of God. This shift in perspective changes the nature of workplace interactions, fostering an environment of mutual support, collaboration, and respect.

The ethical dimension of work also pushes us to think beyond our immediate circles. It encourages us to consider the global impact of our work, especially in relation to issues of poverty and environmental stewardship. As Christians, we're called to a higher purpose than mere consumption; we're called to contribute to the health and well-being of our planet and to seek justice for the oppressed and marginalized.

Indeed, the call to integrate our faith with our work is a high calling. It requires vigilance, courage, and a heart firmly rooted in God's word. It demands that we not only seek personal success but also strive to manifest the values of the Kingdom of God in every endeavor we undertake.

In essence, the ethical dimension of work is about seeing our labor through the lens of faith. It's about understanding that each task, no matter how small, is an opportunity to glorify God, serve our neighbors, and participate in the sacred act of creation. It's a call to live out our faith boldly in the public square, using our vocations as platforms to bear witness to the love and justice of God.

As we navigate the complexities and challenges of integrating our work with our faith, let us draw strength from the community of believers worldwide. Let us encourage one another to pursue excellence, not for our glory but for the glorification of God. Let us remember that in all things, including our professional lives, we are called to manifest the love of Christ, acting justly, loving mercy, and walking humbly with our God.

In conclusion, the ethical dimension of work is not merely an aspect of Christian living; it is at its very core. It reflects our understanding of God's creation, His providence, and His call on our lives. As we go forth in our various vocations, let us do so with a deep sense of purpose and a commitment to ethical integrity, knowing that our work is a vital part of our worship and our witness in the world.

Christian Perspectives on Wealth and Poverty

In navigating the complex terrain of wealth and poverty, Christians are called to a profound and reflective journey that intertwines their faith deeply with the tangible aspects of their everyday lives. Within the Christian tradition, wealth is not condemned; rather, it's the love of money—a root of all kinds of evil—that believers are cautioned against. Here, the essence of stewardship emerges as a vital principle, urging followers to recognize everything they possess as temporary holdings, entrusted to them by God for the betterment of His creation. It's in this light that poverty is not merely seen as a societal ill to be eradicated, but more profoundly, as an invitation to live out the gospel command to love one's neighbor. By weaving the threads of generosity, justice, and humility, Christians are inspired to engage with wealth and poverty in a manner that reflects God's kingdom here on earth. This transformative approach challenges believers to not just offer charity, but also to question and change the structures that perpetuate poverty, thereby embodying a faith that actively seeks to usher in a world of equity and dignity for all.

Stewardship of Resources and the Environment

In the serenity of God's creation, one finds not only beauty and sustenance but also a profound responsibility laid upon the shoulders of humanity. This stewardship, a sacred trust between the Creator and those created in His image, calls for a thoughtful and considerate approach to the resources and environment entrusted to our care. The call to stewardship is not a burden, but a privilege—a chance to reflect God's love and care for all creation.

Scripture speaks volumes on the responsibility humans have towards the earth and its resources. From the verdant gardens of Eden where the first mandate to tend and keep was given, to the poetic praises of creation in the Psalms, the biblical narrative weaves a consistent thread: the earth is the Lord's, and all that is in it. Hence, our interaction with the environment is an act of worship, a testament to our reverence for the Creator.

The concept of stewardship extends beyond mere conservation. It encompasses a holistic approach that integrates respect for ecological systems, sustainable living, and equitable resource distribution. It's a call to live intentionally, considering the impact of our choices on the generations to come. It prompts us to ask: Are we being faithful stewards of God's creation?

In today's world, where consumption often precedes contemplation, embracing stewardship offers a countercultural narrative. It challenges the disposability mindset, urging Christians to adopt lifestyles and practices that harmonize with creation's rhythm. Whether it's reducing waste, supporting sustainable practices, or advocating for policies that protect the environment, the paths to stewardship are as varied as they are vital.

Stewardship of resources also fosters a sense of community and interdependence. The realization that resources are finite and should be shared equitably drives the pursuit of justice for all creation. It leads to the understanding that caring for the environment is intricately connected to loving our neighbor. Whether it is ensuring access to clean water, promoting fair trade, or combatting climate change, stewardship has profound social implications.

The beauty of stewardship lies in its ability to bring about transformation—of hearts, communities, and the environment. It's a journey of learning to live in harmony with creation, adopting practices that heal and restore, rather than deplete and destroy. This journey doesn't demand perfection but progression. It invites small, consistent steps towards a more sustainable and equitable world.

The role of the Church in advocating and practicing stewardship cannot be overstated. As a community of believers, the Church has the opportunity to model stewardship in its operations, teachings, and outreach. Encouraging environmental awareness, supporting green initiatives, and fostering discussions on sustainability can catalyze change within and beyond the church walls.

Education plays a crucial role in cultivating a stewardship ethos. From Sunday schools to seminaries, the Biblical foundation for stewardship and practical ways to care for the environment can be integrated into the curriculum. By instilling values of stewardship in the young, the Church can raise a generation that prioritizes care for creation as an expression of their faith.

Moreover, stewardship of resources also encompasses the wise management of personal and church finances. It advocates for generosity and the use of resources in a way that reflects God's kingdom priorities. It challenges the idolatry of materialism, promoting a lifestyle of contentment and simplicity. Through this, believers can witness to the world a way of life that values creation and community over consumption.

The challenges to environmental stewardship are many, including political, economic, and cultural obstacles. Yet, the call to stewardship remains undiminished. It is a call to courage, to confront these challenges with faith and determination, trusting in God to guide and sustain our efforts.

Partnerships with organizations committed to environmental protection and sustainability can amplify the Church's impact in stewardship efforts. Collaborating on projects, sharing resources, and learning from each other's experiences can foster a collaborative spirit that transcends denominational boundaries.

Prayer and reflection are integral to the stewardship journey. Seeking God's guidance, discerning His will, and being open to the Holy Spirit's leading are essential as we navigate the complexities of environmental ethics. Prayer grounds our actions in God's purposes, ensuring that our efforts in stewardship are aligned with His will.

The rewards of stewardship are manifold—restored ecosystems, strengthened communities, and a deeper communion with our Creator. As we walk this path, we discover the joy of living in a way that honours God and His creation. This journey of stewardship, though challenging, is marked by hope. Hope that our collective efforts can effect change. Hope that future generations will inherit a world where the beauty and bounty of creation are preserved and respected.

Concluding, the stewardship of resources and the environment is a labyrinthine task, which calls for wisdom, commitment, and above all, love. Love for God, love for our neighbor, and love for the creation God has entrusted to us. As we embark on this sacred duty, let us do so with the assurance that our labor is not in vain, for we serve a God who delights in restoration and renewal. May our stewardship reflect the beauty of the Creator, drawing all closer to the One who made heaven and earth.

In embracing stewardship, we follow in the footsteps of Jesus, who lived in harmony with creation, taught parables of seeds and soil, and reminded us that not a sparrow falls without the Father's notice. Let our stewardship be a living parable, a testament to our faith in a Creator who calls us to lovingly care for all He has made.

Chapter 8:
Ethics and Technology

In a world where technology evolves at an unprecedented pace, Christians are faced with new and intricate ethical dilemmas. As we navigate through the dense fog of technological advances, from social media to artificial intelligence, it becomes imperative to anchor our decisions in the steadfast love and wisdom of Christ. How do we discern the benefits and pitfalls of technology while striving to maintain our relationships and communities in this digital age? This chapter delves into the moral complexities that technology introduces into our lives, aiming to equip believers with a framework for making informed, ethical choices that reflect our calling as followers of Jesus. It's not just about deciphering right from wrong; it's about understanding how our technological engagements can either hinder or enhance our spiritual growth and mission. Through a blend of biblical insights and practical wisdom, we'll explore how to use technology in a way that strengthens our bonds with one another, fosters genuine community, and glorifies God in every click, swipe, and post. Let us journey together in wisdom, embracing the opportunities technology offers while guarding our hearts against its potential to distract and divide.

Navigating the Moral Complexities of the Digital Age

In this era, where technology has become a pivotal aspect of our daily lives, Christians are called upon to navigate through the digital mire with a firm grip on their moral compass. The integration of technology in our lives isn't inherently negative; however, the manner in which we engage with digital tools can present complex moral dilemmas that weren't contemplated by previous generations. This chapter aims to shed light on these issues and offer guidance grounded in Christian ethics.

The digital sphere is vast, encompassing social media, forums, blogs, news outlets, and much more. It's a place where opinions are shared freely, sometimes without the filters of kindness, truth, or love that Christianity teaches us to use. How can we, as Christians, ensure that our digital footprint reflects our values? It starts with self-reflection and a commitment to embodying Christ-like behavior online, just as we strive to do offline.

One of the primary concerns in the digital age is the preservation of truth. The internet is rife with misinformation and deception. As followers of Christ, who is the way, the truth, and the life, we are called to be beacons of truth in a sea of falsehoods. This means not only being cautious about the information we share but also dedicating ourselves to seeking out the truth, even when it's not popular or convenient.

Privacy is another significant issue in the digital realm. With the convenience of online platforms comes the risk of oversharing personal information, not just our own but also that of others. The concept of loving our neighbor as ourselves extends to respecting their privacy and dignity online. It's essential to discern what should be shared and what should remain private before hitting that 'share' or 'post' button.

Moreover, the digital age has transformed the way we form and maintain relationships. Though technology can bridge gaps between individuals across the globe, it can also create distances among those physically close to us. The challenge lies in using digital tools to enhance rather than hinder our real-life relationships. Striking a balance where technology serves as a tool for connection, not isolation, is critical.

The rise of digital platforms has also brought about the ease of economic transactions. However, this convenience comes with moral considerations, such as the ethical implications of online shopping practices, cryptocurrency investments, and the digital divide that privileges some while disadvantaging others. Christians are urged to approach these aspects of digital life with a consciousness of stewardship, generosity, and justice.

Moreover, the pervasiveness of technology invites questions about the stewardship of time. With limitless information and entertainment at our fingertips, Christian individuals must exercise discipline to ensure that their time is spent in ways that honor God and foster growth. This includes making conscious choices about the media we consume and the amount of time we devote to digital devices.

Technology has also introduced new avenues for witnessing and spreading the Gospel. Utilizing digital tools for evangelism presents unique opportunities and challenges. Engaging in online ministry requires wisdom, discernment, and an understanding of the digital culture, ensuring that the message of Christ's love is communicated effectively and respectfully.

Furthermore, the anonymity and distance provided by the digital world can sometimes lead to a lack of accountability. Christians are reminded that God's omnipresence extends to the online realm. Our actions, words, and choices on digital platforms should reflect a life lived in awe of God's omniscience and a desire to glorify Him in all things.

Cyberbullying and online harassment are stark examples of the misuse of technology. Christians are called to stand against such behavior, promoting kindness, empathy, and compassion. This entails not only refraining from participating in harmful online activities but also actively advocating for those who are victims of such behaviors.

Protecting the vulnerable extends into the digital world as well. The anonymity and accessibility of the internet have unfortunately facilitated exploitation and harmful content. Christians have a duty to protect themselves and others, especially children and the vulnerable, from these dangers by supporting measures that promote online safety and decency.

Additionally, the digital age poses challenges to mental health, with issues like social media addiction and cyberbullying affecting individuals' well-being. Christians are encouraged to cultivate a healthy digital environment, promoting content that uplifts and edifies, and to foster real-life community connections that offer support and love.

Finally, it's important to remember that while technology continually evolves, the timeless principles of Christianity remain unchanging. The virtues of love, patience, kindness, self-control, and faithfulness are as applicable online as they are offline. As we tread through the complexities of the digital age, let these virtues guide our digital engagements.

As Christians in a digital age, we are navigators in uncharted territories, but we are not without a compass. The teachings of Christ and the principles of Christian ethics light our way. By embodying these values in our digital interactions, we contribute to a more truthful, respectful, and loving online environment.

In conclusion, navigating the moral complexities of the digital age requires constant vigilance, prayer, and a commitment to applying Christian principles in every click, post, and interaction. It's a journey that challenges us to grow in our faith, to reflect Christ in the digital realm, and to inspire others to do the same. With God's guidance, we can face these challenges with confidence and grace, making a positive impact in the digital world for His glory.

The Impact of Technology on Relationships and Community

In navigating the moral complexities of the digital age, one can't help but observe the profound impact technology has had on human interactions and community life. It's a double-edged sword that, while offering unprecedented opportunities for connection, also poses significant challenges to our relationships and social fabric. This chapter delves into these challenges and explores pathways for individuals, especially those guided by Christian principles, to foster genuine connections in an increasingly digital world.

The advent of social media and digital communication tools was heralded as a new dawn for human connectivity. Suddenly, maintaining relationships across vast distances became easier. However, this ease of connection has also led to an unintended paradox — while we're connected more than ever, the depth and quality of these connections can be shallow. Today's challenge lies in discerning how to use these tools without sacrificing the substance of our relationships.

Christian ethics, rooted in the teachings of Scripture, places immense value on community and relationships. "For where two or three gather in my name, there am I with them" (Matthew 18:20), underscores the importance of physical presence and fellowship. In this light, technology should serve as a means to enhance, not replace, face-to-face interactions that are fundamental to building strong, supportive communities.

The consumerist mindset that permeates the digital landscape often treats relationships as commodities — to be 'liked', 'followed', or 'friended' with a click. Yet, in the Christian tradition, relationships are sacred, built on the foundations of love, mutual respect, and commitment. It is vital to approach our digital interactions with the intention of cultivating these values, rather than succumbing to the superficial engagement metrics promoted by social media platforms.

Moreover, the anonymity and physical detachment offered by online platforms can sometimes lead to a breakdown in social norms and respectful discourse. Cyberbullying, trolling, and other forms of harassment can severely damage individuals' mental and emotional well-being. As Christians, we're called to embody Christ's love in all interactions, which includes the digital space. This means engaging in conversations with kindness, patience, and understanding, standing against online harassment, and offering support to those affected.

Another area where technology has altered community dynamics is in the realm of information sharing. The spread of misinformation and 'echo chambers' can further entrench divisions within communities. It becomes imperative, then, to approach the information we share and consume cautiously and critically, always seeking out truth and promoting unity over division.

Digital technology also holds the potential to support community-building efforts, particularly in reaching out to those in need. Online platforms can facilitate the organization of charity events, mobilize resources for disaster relief, and connect individuals seeking to volunteer with opportunities. In embracing these opportunities, we harness technology for the common good, embodying the principle of stewardship entrusted to us.

It's also worth noting the role of technology in supporting families and marriages. While digital devices can sometimes serve as distractions that isolate family members, used wisely, they can support family connections. Setting boundaries around device usage, prioritizing face-to-face interactions during meals and gatherings, and using technology to share in activities can strengthen family bonds.

For church communities, technology opens up new avenues for fellowship and outreach. Online services, prayer groups, and study sessions allow individuals who might be physically unable to attend church to participate in spiritual life. However, these should complement, not substitute, the irreplaceable experience of worshipping and gathering in person.

Community engagement and service can also benefit from thoughtful use of technology. By leveraging digital tools, churches and Christian organizations can more effectively coordinate community initiatives, engage with those they serve, and foster a sense of belonging and involvement among members.

In conclusion, technology's impact on relationships and community need not be viewed solely as a challenge; it also presents opportunities. The key lies in intentional and discerning use, guided by Christian values. By putting emphasis on personal, face-to-face interactions, embodying Christ's love online, seeking truth, and using digital tools for service and connection, we can navigate the complexities of the digital age while enriching our relationships and communities.

As we move forward, let us remember that technology is a tool, and like any tool, its value and impact depend on how we use it. Informed by our faith and guided by compassion, understanding, and love, we can use technology to enhance our lives, deepen our relationships, and strengthen our communities. The digital age offers both challenges and opportunities; by facing them with wisdom and grace, we can forge meaningful connections that transcend the digital divide.

Ultimately, our journey through the digital landscape is not a solitary one. It is a collective endeavor, shaped by our shared values and mutual support. Let us approach it with a spirit of curiosity and openness, always anchored in the teachings of Christ, and strive to create a digital environment that reflects the best of who we are as a community of faith.

Chapter 9:
Social Justice and the Common Good

In the journey of faith, our actions and convictions in the public square are as vital as those within the sanctuary's walls. Chapter 9, "Social Justice and the Common Good," delves into the heart of what it means to live out our Christian calling in the broader context of society. At its core, social justice from a Christian perspective isn't a fleeting trend but a profound commitment to seeing God's justice and love manifested in the world around us. It challenges us to consider not just our own well-being, but the common good—how our lives, choices, and voices can contribute to a reality where every individual experiences the dignity, respect, and opportunity that God desires for His creation.

This chapter unpacks how understanding justice through the lens of Christian faith compels us to advocacy and action, not as an optional add-on to our faith, but as an essential expression of it. It's about recognizing that every person is made in the image of God and therefore deserves to live free from oppression, want, and fear. The role of Christians in advocating for social change is not to impose a theocracy but to demonstrate what it means to love our neighbors as ourselves—whether that's through addressing systemic injustices, caring for the poor, or stewarding the environment. It invites us into a journey of transformation, both personal and societal, guided by the timeless truths of scripture and the radical example of Jesus Christ, who proclaimed good news to the poor, freedom for the oppressed, and the year of the Lord's favor.

Understanding Justice from a Christian Perspective

Embarking on a journey to understand justice through a Christian lens enlightens us not only about the world around us but also about the nature of God and His intentions for humanity. In the heart of Christianity lies the profound understanding that justice is not merely a concept to be debated in courts or philosophical texts, but a divine mandate that permeates every aspect of human existence. It's our compass in navigating the complexities of life, steering us toward actions that echo God's love and righteousness.

The Biblical narrative introduces us to the idea of justice as central to God's character. He is described as just and righteous, qualities that aren't abstract but rather reflected in His dealings with mankind. From the laws given to Moses to the teachings of Jesus, the Scriptures consistently highlight God's concern for fairness, equity, and liberation for the oppressed. This divine perspective on justice can challenge us, as followers of Christ, to look beyond our preconceptions and towards a more holistic understanding of what it means to live justly.

Justice from a Christian viewpoint is inherently tied to the concept of the common good. It compels us to consider not only our individual well-being but also how our actions impact the broader community. This echoes the teachings of Jesus, particularly in His emphasis on loving one's neighbor as oneself. Herein lies a call to action, not just for personal righteousness but for societal transformation that reflects God's kingdom on earth.

Understanding justice in this light demands a reflection on the role of grace and forgiveness. Unlike a human system of justice that often focuses on retribution, God's justice is restorative at its core. It seeks to redeem rather than just punish, to restore relationships rather than merely enforce laws. This doesn't negate the need for accountability but frames it within a context of love and redemption.

The pursuit of justice, therefore, becomes a profound act of faith. It's about trusting that our efforts to act justly are part of a larger divine plan for humanity. It is recognizing that justice is not just an end but a means through which we experience and manifest God's grace in the world. As Christians, the challenge is to continuously ask ourselves how our actions contribute to the realization of God's justice on earth.

Embodying justice also means embracing humility and listening. In a world that often champions the loudest voices, the Christian perspective on justice involves listening to those who are marginalized and oppressed, understanding their experiences, and advocating for change. It's about embodying the empathy and compassion that Jesus showed to those who were often overlooked or undervalued by society.

This concept of justice further calls for a reevaluation of power and privilege. The Gospel challenges us to use whatever power or resources we have not for our own benefit alone but in service of others, especially the most vulnerable. This aligns with the biblical understanding of stewardship, where everything we have is considered a trust from God to be used in alignment with His purposes.

In practical terms, living out justice involves both individual and collective action. It can be as personal as making ethical choices in our daily lives, or as public as advocating for policies that correct injustices in society. It requires discernment to know when to speak, when to act, and when to simply stand in solidarity with those fighting for their rights.

Moreover, the pursuit of justice must be sustained by a deep spiritual rootedness. Just as Jesus often withdrew to pray and commune with the Father, our efforts to act justly should be undergirded by a vibrant spiritual life. This not only fortifies us for the long haul but keeps our motives and methods anchored in love.

The challenge, however, is that the path of justice is often met with resistance. It can be a lonely road, fraught with misunderstanding and opposition. Yet, the biblical narrative is filled with stories of individuals who, empowered by their faith, confronted injustice courageously. These stories offer both inspiration and a reminder that the pursuit of justice, even when difficult, is integral to the Christian witness.

As we contemplate the role of justice in our lives and communities, it's crucial to remember that our efforts are not in vain. The Bible assures us that the arc of the moral universe, though long, bends towards justice. This doesn't merely offer comfort but energizes our commitment to seeking justice in the present, trusting in the eventual fulfillment of God's just kingdom.

In conclusion, understanding justice from a Christian perspective invites us into a dynamic and transformative journey. It encourages us to look beyond mere human law to the heart of divine law, where love and justice meet. As we navigate this journey, may we be guided by the wisdom of the Scriptures, the example of Jesus, and the prompting of the Holy Spirit. Let us strive to be agents of justice, bearers of light in a world yearning for righteousness and peace.

Let this understanding spur us on to live lives marked by justice, empowered by faith, and enriched by the grace and truth that define our walk with Christ. May our pursuit of justice reflect the heart of God, moving us ever closer to the reality of His kingdom on earth as it is in heaven.

In embracing this calling, let us remember that our actions, both great and small, contribute to the tapestry of God's redemptive work in the world. Our pursuit of justice, therefore, is not just an obligation but a privilege, inviting us into deeper fellowship with God and one another as we seek to embody His love and righteousness in all that we do. May we step forward in faith, courage, and hope, trusting that our efforts are part of a larger divine orchestration towards a just and equitable world.

The Role of Christians in Advocating for Social Change

In the mosaic of human history, the influence of Christianity on the moral and ethical fabric of society is both vast and nuanced. As followers of Christ, Christians are called not only to personal transformation but also to be catalysts for change in the world around them. This calling places a responsibility on Christians to advocate for social justice and the common good, to be the voice for the voiceless, and to stand up against injustices whenever and wherever they arise.

The foundation of advocating for social change as Christians lies in understanding the inherent dignity and worth of every individual, created in the image of God. This profound recognition fuels our pursuit of justice, guiding us to confront systems of oppression and inequality. It compels us to challenge societal norms that marginalize the weak and exploit the vulnerable, for in every face we seek to see the face of Christ himself.

However, the path of advocacy is no easy journey. It requires courage, perseverance, and a deep-rooted faith that believes in the transformative power of love and justice. Christians are called to be the salt of the earth, a preservative force against decay and a flavor that brings out the God-given goodness in the world. Likewise, as the light of the world, we are to illuminate dark places, exposing injustice and bringing hope.

The role of prayer in advocacy cannot be overstated. Prayer aligns our hearts with God's heart, giving us His compassion for the oppressed and His passion for justice. It is in the place of prayer that we find the strength to stand firm, the wisdom to advocate effectively, and the grace to love even our adversaries.

Actively engaging with our communities allows Christians to put their faith into action. Whether it's participating in local government, supporting organizations that fight inequality, or simply standing alongside those who are being treated unfairly, every action counts. Social change often starts with small acts of kindness and solidarity.

Educating oneself about the issues facing our society today is another critical step. Understanding the complexities of poverty, racism, environmental degradation, and other forms of injustice enables Christians to advocate more effectively. It also helps in dismantling harmful stereotypes and prejudices that often cloud our judgment and actions.

Christians are also uniquely positioned to build bridges where there are divisions. By demonstrating Christ's love to everyone—friend or foe—we embody a powerful alternative to the hatred and bitterness that fuel so much of the world's strife. This reconciliatory stance is a testament to the reality that in Christ, there is neither Jew nor Gentile, slave nor free, male nor female.

The teachings of Jesus in the Sermon on the Mount provide a blueprint for Christian advocacy. He blessed the peacemakers, the merciful, and those who hunger and thirst for righteousness. These beatitudes call Christians to a radical lifestyle of advocacy and peacemaking, rooted in mercy and a relentless pursuit of righteousness.

Scripture is replete with examples of God's concern for justice and equity. The prophets, in particular, bear witness to God's demand for social righteousness and care for the marginalized. Christians, therefore, have a rich biblical heritage that undergirds their advocacy for social change, providing both inspiration and instruction.

Community engagement is another key aspect of advocating for social change. By building relationships with those who are different from us, we can begin to understand the challenges they face and stand in solidarity with them. Furthermore, these relationships can transcend cultural and social barriers, showcasing the unifying power of Christ's love.

The pursuit of social justice also involves advocating for systemic change. This means challenging unfair laws and policies and working toward the creation of more equitable systems. Christians can influence social policy by voting, lobbying, and even running for office, guided by their moral compass and commitment to the common good.

Yet, in all our efforts, we must remember that our ultimate trust is not in human institutions but in God, who is the source of all justice and righteousness. Our advocacy should be marked by humility, recognizing that we too are flawed and in need of God's grace. This humility allows us to engage in social change efforts with compassion and empathy, rather than judgment or self-righteousness.

In conclusion, the role of Christians in advocating for social change is multifaceted and deeply rooted in the teachings and example of Jesus Christ. It involves prayer, action, education, community engagement, and systemic advocacy, all done in the spirit of humility and love. By embracing this calling, Christians can make a significant impact on their communities and the world, reflecting God's kingdom of justice, peace, and love.

As we stand at the crossroads of faith and social action, let us choose the path of advocacy, emboldened by our faith and inspired by the love of Christ. For in seeking justice for others, we find a deeper understanding of God's heart and our own purpose in His divine plan.

Chapter 10:
Tolerance, Christian Mission, and Coexistence

In our journey through the complexities of Christian ethics, we arrive at a pivotal point: the exploration of tolerance, Christian mission, and coexistence. This chapter delves into the essence of tolerance viewed through a Christian lens, emphasizing that it isn't about compromising our faith but about meeting others with the love and respect that Jesus demonstrated. The challenge we confront in a pluralistic society isn't about diluting our beliefs but about how we live out our faith among people of different beliefs without losing our distinctiveness as followers of Christ. This delicate balance requires us to be as shrewd as serpents and as innocent as doves, navigating the fine line between upholding our principles and engaging with the world around us in a way that reflects God's love.

The mission we have been entrusted with is not merely about proclamation but also about living in a manner that draws others to Christ. This calls for a deep-rooted tolerance that does not equate to acceptance of all ideas as equal but recognizes the dignity of each person made in the image of God. The task at hand involves creating spaces where genuine dialogue can occur, places where the Gospel can be shared not as a weapon of division but as an invitation to love. As we move forward, let's remember that our call to coexistence is not a mandate to blur the lines of our faith but to stand firmly within its bounds, extending a hand of friendship to all, knowing that in the diversity of God's creation, there's room for meaningful and transformative encounters.

Defining Tolerance in a Christian Context

In the tapestry of human interaction, the virtue of tolerance acts as a delicate thread binding the mosaic of cultures, beliefs, and perspectives together in a pursuit of peace and understanding. Within the Christian ethos, tolerance is not merely a societal expectation but an expression of the divine command to love our neighbors as ourselves. As we embark on exploring tolerance through a Christian lens, it's crucial to grasp that this virtue, deeply rooted in the biblical narrative, requires us to extend grace, respect, and love to those around us, even when we encounter stark differences.

To define tolerance in a Christian context is to recognize it as a balance between truth and love. It's an acknowledgment that while we steadfastly hold onto our convictions, our interactions and responses to those of differing beliefs should be characterized by compassion and understanding. This balance reflects Jesus' own approach to those he met, where he offered grace without compromising on truth.

It's important to highlight that Christian tolerance does not equate to relativism or the dilution of beliefs. Instead, it's an invitation to engage respectfully and thoughtfully with the world around us while firmly rooted in our faith. This approach challenges us to look beyond the surface and see the image of God in every person we encounter, driving us toward meaningful dialogue and mutual respect.

Furthermore, Christian tolerance compels us to examine our attitudes towards those who oppose or object to our faith. The New Testament is replete with teachings that encourage us to respond with kindness and gentility, even in the face of hostility. This is not a call to passivity but to an active pursuit of peace, rooted in strength and confidence in our convictions.

The parables and teachings of Jesus offer profound insights into the nature of tolerance. Stories such as the Good Samaritan serve as powerful reminders that love and compassion often transcend the boundaries of culture, religion, and societal norms. These teachings encourage us to extend a hand of friendship and understanding across divides, building bridges where walls once stood.

Practicing tolerance within a Christian framework is about embodying the fruits of the Spirit in our interactions with others. As we let love, joy, peace, patience, kindness, goodness, faithfulness, gentleness, and self-control guide us, our capacity for tolerance grows. This spiritual transformation enables us to navigate disagreements and conflicts with grace and wisdom.

It is also essential to understand that tolerance, as envisioned by Christianity, has its limits. When tolerance is misconstrued as acceptance of actions that are unequivocally condemned by scripture, we must discern where to draw the line. Here, the Christian's role is not to judge but to uphold truth while maintaining a spirit of love and humility. This delicate balance requires constant prayer, reflection, and a deep reliance on the Holy Spirit for guidance.

In practicing Christian tolerance, we are called to be ambassadors for Christ, demonstrating what it means to live a life marked by love and grace. This, however, does not mean shying away from sharing our faith. On the contrary, it's through our loving tolerance that the beauty of the gospel shines brightest, drawing others towards the transformative power of Christ's love.

The community of believers plays a pivotal role in fostering an environment of tolerance. Churches should be sanctuaries of acceptance, where diverse backgrounds and perspectives are not just tolerated but celebrated. This unity in diversity reflects the kingdom of God and serves as a testament to the power of Christian love in overcoming division.

Moreover, Christian education on the subject of tolerance is paramount. By grounding our understanding of tolerance in biblical teachings, we equip ourselves and future generations to navigate the complexities of our pluralistic world with wisdom and integrity. This education should inspire not only intellectual assent but a heartfelt commitment to embodying tolerance in our daily lives.

In the pursuit of tolerance, forgiveness is a key element. The gospel calls us to forgive as we have been forgiven, a principle that directly impacts our ability to practice tolerance. By letting go of grievances and choosing to forgive, we open the doors to reconciliation and mutual understanding.

Finally, it's worth emphasizing that tolerance, in the Christian sense, is an active virtue. It involves listening earnestly, speaking truth in love, and standing alongside those in need, regardless of their beliefs. It's about making the conscious choice to see the humanity in the other, even when the world urges us to focus on our differences.

In conclusion, defining tolerance in a Christian context is to navigate the tension between holding firm to our beliefs while engaging the world with compassion and understanding. It's a call to action, urging us to reflect the love of Christ in every interaction and to bridge divides with the healing power of grace. As we walk this path, let us be guided by the Holy Spirit, drawing on the strength and wisdom that comes from our faith, and shine as beacons of tolerance in a world yearning for peace and understanding.

As we move forward, bearing in mind the complexities and nuances of tolerance, may our journey be marked by an unwavering commitment to embodying the values of Christ's kingdom. Let our lives be testament to the transformative power of Christian tolerance, paving the way for a world where love triumphs over division, and understanding overcomes prejudice. In doing so, we fulfill our mission, not just as followers of Christ, but as advocates for a more tolerant, loving, and peaceful world.

The Challenge of Living Faithfully in a Pluralistic Society

In today's dynamic world, the Christian walk is akin to navigating a river's currents, where the waters of pluralism and moral relativism flow strongly and often contrary to the teachings of Scripture. This journey, while challenging, offers profound opportunities for personal growth and witness. Christians are called not only to exist within this pluralistic society but to thrive, bringing the light of Christ to diverse communities. But how can we live out our faith authentically while respecting those whose beliefs differ vastly from our own?

First, it's essential to recognize the value of pluralism as a testing ground for our faith. It sharpens our understanding and articulation of what we believe. As iron sharpens iron, so too does engaging with a variety of perspectives hone our ability to communicate the Gospel effectively. It's not about watering down our beliefs, but rather, understanding them so deeply that we can engage in meaningful dialogue with others.

Understanding that tolerance does not mean agreement is a crucial distinction in this journey. As believers, we are called to love our neighbors, irrespective of their beliefs. This form of radical love doesn't require us to relinquish our convictions but to hold them with humility, recognizing that our first allegiance is to Christ and His command to love.

One practical step for living faithfully in a pluralistic society is to cultivate deep, genuine relationships with those outside our faith tradition. This involves listening intently, seeking to understand before being understood, and showing Christ's love through actions, not just words. It's in the context of relationships that the authenticity of our faith shines brightest and becomes most attractive.

Engaging with the culture rather than withdrawing from it is another critical aspect of this challenge. Jesus prayed not for His disciples to be taken out of the world but for their protection and witness within it (John 17). Our call is to be in the world, engaging with it thoughtfully, creatively, and courageously, shining as lights in darkness.

It's also imperative to recognize the importance of spiritual disciplines in living faithfully. Regular prayer, meditation on Scripture, and participation in community worship are not just personal edification tools but fuel for our mission in the world. These practices ground us in God's truth and empower us to navigate the complexities of a pluralistic society with wisdom and grace.

Furthermore, embracing the diversity within the body of Christ itself is a powerful witness to the world. A church that reflects the unity and diversity of its members is a testament to the gospel's transcultural power. It preaches louder than words that in Christ, there is neither Jew nor Gentile, slave nor free, male nor female (Galatians 3:28)—all are one.

Navigating ethical and moral dilemmas with a biblical lens while respecting others' views requires wisdom that God promises to give generously (James 1:5). It's about seeking His guidance daily and being open to the Holy Spirit's leading on how to act justly, love mercy, and walk humbly with Him (Micah 6:8).

Moreover, being informed about the beliefs and values of others is not just useful but necessary. Misunderstandings about what others believe can lead to fear and division. By educating ourselves, we can engage in conversations that are respectful and informed, pointing toward the truth with gentleness and respect.

Practitioners of hospitality in a diverse society, Christians are called to open their homes, churches, and lives as spaces where honest conversations about faith can occur. It's within the framework of hospitality that barriers break down and the Gospel can be shared authentically and effectively.

Commitment to the truth of the Gospel, paired with an attitude of grace, builds bridges. Our witness in a pluralistic society should be marked by a compelling blend of truth and love, standing firm in our convictions while demonstrating the grace that has been shown to us.

Living faithfully in a pluralistic society is not just about staying afloat amidst the currents of competing ideologies but about setting our sails to catch the wind of the Spirit, leading conversations and actions that draw others into the irresistible grace of Christ. It's a journey that requires boldness, humility, and a deep reliance on God's power and wisdom.

In conclusion, as we navigate the challenge of living out our faith in a pluralistic society, let's remember that our ultimate goal isn't to win arguments but to win souls. By embodying the love, truth, and grace of Christ, we can be beacons of hope in a divided world, demonstrating the transformative power of the Gospel in our lives and communities.

May we lean into this challenge, recognizing it as an opportunity to grow in faith and witness. Through God's grace and guidance, we can live lives that not only navigate the challenges of pluralism but flourish within them, drawing others to the light and love of Christ.

Chapter 11:
Forgiveness and Reconciliation

In navigating life's complex web, the power of forgiveness and the journey towards reconciliation emerge as bedrock principles within Christian ethics, offering a path to transform both hearts and relationships. It's not just about moving past an offense but engaging in a transformative process that reflects the profound mercy and love demonstrated through Jesus Christ. This chapter delves into the critical importance of forgiveness, not as a mere formality but as a deeply personal act that liberates the soul and mends the fabric of community. Here, practical guidance for fostering reconciliation is woven with the understanding that true peace is never a surface-level truce but a heartfelt commitment to rebuild trust and understanding, even in the face of deep wounds. As Christians, the call to extend forgiveness is not optional but a mandate that mirrors divine grace, recognizing that reconciliation's road may be steeped in prayer, patience, and often, profound courage. Unlocking the profound strength found in forgiveness and the subsequent repair of fractured bonds exemplifies the heart of Christian living, offering a testament to the world of the transformative power of love in action.

The Importance of Forgiveness in Christian Ethics

In the journey through Christian ethics, the path of forgiveness stands as a cornerstone, shaping not only the way we interact with each other but how we align ourselves with God's will. The essence of forgiveness in Christian ethics cannot be overstated; it is a pivotal theme that reverberates through scripture, tradition, and personal transformation. Embracing forgiveness is more than an act of letting go; it's an act of profound love that mirrors the character of God.

Forgiveness is integral to the fabric of Christian life, teaching us to release resentment and embrace peace. At its heart, forgiveness is a divine command, a call to embody the grace and mercy that God freely offers to all. It's about breaking the chains of anger and bitterness that tether us to the past, allowing us to move forward with a spirit of compassion and humility.

The power of forgiveness is transformative. It rebuilds broken relationships, restores hope, and heals wounds. This process is not merely about acknowledging wrongs but actively seeking to mend the breach, to restore unity. Through forgiveness, we open the door to reconciliation, paving the way for genuine healing and understanding.

The centrality of forgiveness in Christian ethics is rooted in the example of Jesus Christ. His teachings and actions underscored forgiveness as foundational to the moral life. Whether through parables like that of the prodigal son or his plea for forgiveness for those who crucified him, Jesus's life is a testament to the boundless capacity for forgiveness.

Christian ethics compel us to view forgiveness not as optional but as essential. It challenges us to forgive as we have been forgiven, to extend grace as we have received grace. This call to forgiveness is not about denying justice or condoning harm. Rather, it's about understanding the redemptive power of forgiveness and its role in facilitating healing and reconciliation.

Practicing forgiveness can be challenging. It requires strength, courage, and vulnerability. It calls for us to put aside our pride, to confront our pain and the pain we have caused. Yet, it is in this space of vulnerability that we find growth and the capacity to understand the depth of God's love for us and our call to love one another.

Forgiveness in Christian ethics goes beyond personal relationships. It has societal implications, pushing us towards a more compassionate and just world. It encourages us to address grievances, seek societal healing, and work towards reconciliation in broader contexts. It presents a counter-narrative to the cycles of vengeance and retribution that often govern human interactions.

Fostering a culture of forgiveness within the Christian community serves as a witness to the world. It demonstrates the power of love over hate, of unity over division. This witness is crucial in a world where forgiveness is often seen as weakness. It's a testament to the strength and resilience of a community grounded in the principles of Christian ethics.

The practice of forgiveness also has profound personal benefits. It liberates us from the bondage of negative emotions and leads us to a place of peace and serenity. It fosters emotional and spiritual growth, deepening our relationship with God and with those around us. By embracing forgiveness, we cultivate a heart of mercy, patience, and understanding.

Moreover, forgiveness is a key to unlocking the door to personal and communal revival. It refreshes our spirits and renews our hearts, making way for the Holy Spirit to work within us and through us. As we let go of grievances, we make room for God's grace to transform us, molding us more into His likeness.

Educating believers on the importance of forgiveness is crucial. Churches and religious leaders have a vital role in guiding their congregations in understanding and practicing forgiveness. Through sermons, Bible studies, and counseling, they can provide the tools and support needed to foster a culture of forgiveness.

The journey towards forgiveness is often complex and multifaceted. It involves prayer, reflection, and sometimes, guidance from others. It's a process that may require time, but with each step, we move closer to healing and wholeness. It's a testament to our faith and our commitment to living out the principles of Christian ethics.

In conclusion, the importance of forgiveness in Christian ethics cannot be overstated. It is a fundamental aspect of our moral and spiritual development. Forgiveness is a divine command that offers a path to healing, reconciliation, and peace. As followers of Christ, we are called to a life of forgiveness, reflecting God's love and grace in our lives and in our world. This journey of forgiveness is challenging yet profoundly rewarding, offering us a glimpse into the heart of God and the transformative power of His love.

As we forge ahead in our exploration of Christian ethics, let us hold fast to the principle of forgiveness. May we embody it in our daily lives, extending grace and mercy to all, and walking in the footsteps of Christ. In doing so, we not only enrich our own lives but contribute to the healing and restoration of the world around us. Forgiveness is not just an ethical imperative; it's a beacon of hope, a testament to the indomitable spirit of love and compassion that defines the essence of our faith.

Practical Steps Toward Reconciliation

In the journey of life, embarking on the path of reconciliation can arguably be one of the most challenging yet rewarding endeavors. It's a process that not only heals but transforms, echoing the essence of Christian teachings. Taking practical steps toward reconciliation ensures that we embody the principles of love and forgiveness, instrumental in mending bonds and fostering unity.

First and foremost, reconciliation begins with self-reflection. It requires us to introspect, identifying our role in the conflict and acknowledging our faults. This inward journey is not for the faint-hearted, as it compels us to confront uncomfortable truths about ourselves. However, it's a critical step, for without recognizing our own faults, true reconciliation cannot be achieved.

Forgiveness is the cornerstone of reconciliation. It's an act of will, a decision to let go of resentment and thoughts of revenge. Remember, forgiving is not about condoning the wrongdoing but about liberating oneself from the grip of harbored negativity. It is, as taught in numerous scriptures, a divine attribute that we, as followers, are encouraged to emulate.

Communication is the bridge that connects two estranged shores. Approaching the other party to express your desire for reconciliation is a brave and crucial step. This interaction must be imbued with humility, honesty, and openness. Speaking from the heart and actively listening to the other side fosters understanding and empathy, essential elements for reconciliation.

Prayer cannot be underestimated in this process. Seeking divine guidance imbues one with the strength, patience, and wisdom required to navigate the murky waters of reconciliation. It's a source of solace and a reminder of the ultimate role model in forgiveness—Jesus Christ.

Setting aside pride is a necessary sacrifice on the altar of reconciliation. Pride often prolongs conflicts, clouding our judgment and feeding our ego at the expense of peace and unity. Embracing humility paves the way for mutual understanding and compromise.

Seeking mediation can also be instrumental. There are instances where the chasm of discord is too wide for the involved parties to bridge on their own. In such cases, the unbiased perspective of a mediator—a respected figure or authority within the community—can facilitate a neutral ground for dialogue.

Taking responsibility and apologizing where necessary signals sincerity and a genuine desire for reconciliation. An apology, however, should not be conditional or expecting of immediate forgiveness. It is an offering of peace, left at the discretion of the other to accept in their own time.

Reconciliation is a journey, not a destination. It's important to be patient and not rush the process. Healing wounds and rebuilding trust take time. Celebrate small victories and progress, no matter how insignificant they may seem. These are the stepping stones towards full restoration of the relationship.

Establishing boundaries and new norms is crucial for ensuring past conflicts do not resurface. It's about learning from previous mistakes and actively working to create a healthier dynamic. These new guidelines provide clarity and a framework for interaction moving forward.

Embrace vulnerability. Opening up about your feelings and fears can be daunting but doing so invites the other party to reciprocate. This mutual vulnerability fosters a deeper connection and understanding, reinforcing the bond that was once fractured.

Forgive yourself. Often, we are our own harshest critics. Holding onto self-blame hinders the healing process. Recognize that making mistakes is part of being human, and forgiving yourself is a step towards inner peace.

Be willing to let go of the relationship if necessary. Sometimes, despite the best efforts, reconciliation may not be possible. This could be due to various factors outside one's control. In such instances, it's crucial to find peace in the attempt and closure in the willingness to move forward.

Finally, keep love at the forefront. The ultimate goal of reconciliation is not merely to resolve a conflict but to restore a relationship through the power of love. Let love guide your actions, words, and thoughts throughout this journey.

In conclusion, the road to reconciliation is paved with challenges but also with immense potential for growth, healing, and renewal. By embracing these practical steps, grounded in Christian ethics, individuals can navigate the complexities of reconciliation. It's a testament to the transformative power of forgiveness and love—a reflection of divine grace in our lives.

Chapter 12:
The Ethical Challenges of Globalization

In an era where our lives are intricately interconnected across continents, globalization presents unique ethical dilemmas that beckon the Christian conscience into deep reflection and action. This vast network of global interaction not only expands opportunities but also magnifies responsibilities, urging us to reconsider the scope of our neighborly love. Here, we delve into the heart of these challenges, facing the harsh realities of global poverty head-on and embracing our role in fostering economic justice from a Christian standpoint. We are called to navigate the rich tapestry of global cultural diversity with grace, understanding that our ethical frameworks must stretch beyond borders, recognizing the image of God in every individual, irrespective of geographic or cultural divides. This chapter aims to equip you with the discernment needed to act justly, love mercy, and walk humbly with God in a world marked by significant disparities and cultural complexities. By integrating biblical principles with global awareness, we find ourselves on a path that not only acknowledges the weight of these ethical challenges but also champions the transformative power of Christian love in action across the globe.

Global Poverty and Christian Responsibility

In our journey through the ethical challenges of globalization, we find ourselves confronting a glaring and persistent issue: global poverty. As followers of Christ, our hearts are stirred not only by the staggering statistics of those living in extreme poverty but by the calling upon our lives to act in response to this crisis. The issue of global poverty reaches deep into the fabric of Christian ethics, challenging us to reflect on our lifestyle, choices, and the principles that guide our interactions with the less fortunate among us.

At its core, the Christian faith is marked by a profound commitment to love and serve the marginalized, the oppressed, and those in need. This commitment is not merely a suggestion but a command that echoes through the pages of Scripture. From the Old Testament teachings on justice and care for the poor to Jesus' own ministry that brought healing, hope, and provision to the least in society, the biblical mandate to care for the poor is undeniable.

Yet, in a world characterized by vast inequalities and systemic injustices, the task of addressing global poverty can feel overwhelming. It's easy to wonder, "What difference can I truly make?" This question, while understandable, underestimates the power of collective action and the transformative potential of living out Christian principles in practical ways. We are called not to solve global poverty on our own but to contribute to a larger movement of compassion and justice that reflects the heart of God.

Engaging with global poverty requires us not only to offer immediate relief to those in need but also to confront the underlying structures that perpetuate poverty. This dual approach involves both acts of charity and advocacy efforts aimed at changing unjust systems. As Christians, we are positioned to leverage our influence, resources, and networks in ways that advocate for policies and practices that uplift the impoverished and marginalized.

One fundamental step in this journey is developing a global mindset that recognizes the interconnectedness of all humanity. In a globalized world, the decisions we make—including how we spend our money, the causes we support, and the way we conduct business—have far-reaching implications. By making conscious, ethical choices that prioritize the welfare of others, we begin to align our lives with the biblical call to love our neighbors as ourselves, regardless of geographical boundaries.

Another critical element is solidarity. Solidarity with the poor means more than simply feeling empathy for their struggles; it entails identifying with them to the extent that their fight against poverty becomes our fight as well. This solidarity is rooted in the recognition of the inherent dignity and worth of every individual, created in the image of God.

Practically speaking, this can manifest in various forms, from supporting mission works and charities focused on poverty alleviation to volunteering our time and talents in service of those in need. It also means educating ourselves and others about the complexities of poverty and advocating for fair trade, debt relief for impoverished nations, and sustainable development practices.

As we contemplate our responsibility as Christians toward the global poor, it's vital to approach this calling with humility and a willingness to learn. While we seek to be agents of change, we must also recognize the limits of our understanding and the importance of listening to those we are seeking to help. True service is not about imposing our solutions but about partnering with communities to empower them toward a better future.

This endeavor also requires perseverance. The fight against global poverty is not one that will be won overnight. There will be setbacks and challenges along the way, but our commitment to this cause must be unwavering. We draw strength from our faith, knowing that our efforts are grounded in the divine mandate to love mercy, act justly, and walk humbly with our God.

Moreover, addressing global poverty as Christians invites us to examine our lives and make necessary changes that reflect our commitment to this cause. This might mean adjusting our lifestyle and consumption habits to reduce waste and ensure that our choices do not inadvertently harm the vulnerable. It also involves a commitment to generosity, not just of our financial resources but of our time and voices in advocating for change.

In the midst of these efforts, it's crucial to find community with others who share this commitment. Working alongside fellow believers, churches, and organizations amplifies our impact and provides the support needed to navigate the complexities of global poverty. Together, we can foster a culture within the Christian community that prioritizes the needs of the poor and models the compassionate, justice-oriented heart of God.

Ultimately, our response to global poverty is a reflection of our understanding of the Gospel. It's an acknowledgment that our faith is not separate from the social realities of our world but deeply entwined with them. As we extend mercy, pursue justice, and embody the love of Christ to the least of these, we bear witness to the transformative power of the Gospel to heal and reconcile a broken world.

In conclusion, the issue of global poverty presents both a challenge and an opportunity for Christians. It's an invitation to live out our faith in ways that are tangible, impactful, and aligned with the heart of God. As we seek to navigate this complex issue, may we do so with wisdom, courage, and a deep-seated love that mirrors the love of Christ for all humanity.

Christian Ethics in the Context of Global Cultural Diversity

In this era of unbridled globalization, we find ourselves at a crossroads of cultural, ethical, and spiritual dimensions that cannot be ignored.

As followers of Christ, we face the imperative to navigate through this rich tapestry with grace, understanding, and an unwavering commitment to the Gospel. The challenge before us is not just to cling to our moral foundations but to engage with the global community in ways that respect and honor the diversity of God's creation.

The Gospel of Christ teaches us about love, acceptance, and compassion. These virtues are not bound by geography, language, or culture. They are universal truths that transcend societal differences. In a world that is increasingly interconnected, our call is to manifest these values in every interaction and decision. This is easier said than done, particularly when confronted with practices and beliefs that starkly contrast with our own. The tension between maintaining our Christian identity while embracing global cultural diversity lies at the heart of the ethical challenges we face today.

Understanding and respect are the cornerstones of navigating this global labyrinth. This does not mean compromising our beliefs but rather seeking to understand where others are coming from. Every culture and religion holds values that echo the teachings of Christ in some form—compassion, altruism, and a sense of community. Recognizing these shared values can serve as a bridge between seemingly disparate worlds, allowing us to engage in meaningful dialogue.

Such dialogue is not just about speaking; it's about listening—truly listening—with an open heart and mind. This can be challenging, especially when we encounter views that conflict with our own. However, it is through this process of exchange and reflection that growth occurs. We are called not to judge but to love and understand, remembering that Christ too engaged with those of different faiths and backgrounds.

Amidst global cultural diversity, ethical dilemmas inevitably arise, necessitating tough decisions. Whether it's the nuances of social justice, environmental stewardship, or economic inequality, the decisions we make must be anchored in our faith while being informed by the complexities of the world around us. Our ethical frameworks should thus be both steadfast and flexible, capable of guiding us in diverse contexts.

The embodiment of Christian ethics in our lives is a powerful testament to our faith. It demonstrates that our principles are not mere abstract concepts but lived realities. This authenticity is critical in a world searching for meaning and truth. By walking our talk, we not only live up to our moral obligations but also inspire others to reflect on their own ethical stances.

Moreover, the pursuit of justice and equity, fundamental tenets of Christian ethics, finds a broader canvas in the global context. Our fight against poverty, discrimination, and exploitation extends beyond our immediate communities. The interconnectedness of our world means that our choices and actions have far-reaching impacts. As Christians, we have a role to play in advocating for change, not only locally but also globally, ensuring that our voices contribute to the chorus calling for a more just and compassionate world.

In embracing global cultural diversity, we must also grapple with the reality of intolerance and persecution. Our response to such challenges is a testament to our faith. It's an opportunity to practice forgiveness, seek reconciliation, and stand firm in our convictions, all while extending the olive branch of peace and understanding.

Admittedly, walking this tightrope between adherence to our faith and openness to the world's diversity can be daunting. It requires wisdom, discernment, and, most importantly, prayer. We must constantly seek God's guidance, asking for the strength to be beacons of His love in a world that often feels fragmented and polarized.

The beauty of Christian ethics in the context of global cultural diversity lies in its ability to adapt and resonate across cultures. While the core Gospel message remains unchanged, its expression can be as varied as humanity itself. This flexibility allows us to connect with others on a profound level, building bridges where walls once stood.

Finally, it's essential to remember that we are not alone in this journey. The global Christian community is a vast network of support, learning, and fellowship. We can draw strength from one another, learning from diverse perspectives and experiences to enrich our understanding and practice of our faith.

In conclusion, the ethical challenges of globalization call us to a deeper engagement with our faith and the world. They invite us to live out the Gospel in ways that honor and respect the diversity of God's creation while staying true to the bedrock of Christian ethics. Through understanding, dialogue, and love, we can traverse the complex landscape of global cultural diversity, guiding by the light of Christ's teachings and the strength of our convictions.

Let us embark on this journey with humility, courage, and faith, knowing that in our diversity lies our strength and in our unity, our hope. The path may be fraught with challenges, but it is also ripe with opportunities—to learn, to grow, and to witness the transformative power of Christ's love in every corner of the globe.

Conclusion

In this journey, we've traversed the breadth and depth of Christian ethics, seeking understanding and guidance for navigating the complexities of daily life through a Christian lens. From the foundational role of scripture and tradition in shaping our moral compass to the practical application of virtues that enrich the human experience, each chapter has been a stepping stone towards a more integrated and holistic approach to living out our faith. We've explored how ethical principles manifest in the sanctity of life, the nuances of family and relationships, and our stewardship of resources, including the profound challenges and opportunities presented by technology and globalization.

Central to this exploration has been the recognition of the ongoing tension between timeless Christian principles and the rapidly evolving moral landscape of our modern world. Yet, within this tension lies our greatest opportunity for witness and service. As we close, let's remember that our calling is not to retreat from the world but to engage with it courageously and compassionately, armed with the wisdom and guidance we've gleaned. The path forward may be fraught with uncertainty and challenge, but it is also ripe with the possibility for transformation—of ourselves and the world around us. Let us then, with grace and conviction, step into our roles as bearers of light and love, contributing to a more just, compassionate, and ethical world.

Book Review Request

If this journey through the exploration of Christian ethics has ignited a flame within you, guiding you towards practical wisdom and deeper reflection, I wholeheartedly invite you to share your experience. Your insights and reflections could serve as beacon lights for others seeking to navigate the complexities of life through a Christian lens. Writing a review could not only enrich your understanding but also inspire a community striving to live out these timeless principles in their daily lives.

Appendix A:|
Appendix

In this journey we've embarked on together, navigating the complexities of integrating Christian moral principles into every facet of our lives, we've covered a broad range of topics. From the grounding of our morals in scripture and tradition to the application of these principles in the modern world, the chapters thus far have aimed to equip you with the tools needed to live out your faith vibrantly in today's society.

Yet, the conversation and the journey do not end here. The quest for understanding and living out Christian ethics is ongoing, constantly evolving as we ourselves grow and as the world around us changes. It's a journey that demands perpetual learning, reflection, and action. With this in mind, Appendix A is designed to be a bridge, leading you toward further resources that can deepen your understanding and enhance your application of Christian ethics.

Resources for Further Study

The realm of Christian ethics is vast, encompassing a wide array of disciplines, perspectives, and methodologies. To continue growing in your knowledge and practice, consider exploring the following types of resources:

1. **Books and Academic Journals:** There's a wealth of scholarly work that delves deeper into the topics we've touched upon.

Looking into books and journals focused on Christian ethics can provide you with a more nuanced understanding of complex issues.

2. **Bible Commentaries and Theological Works:** To further ground your ethical decisions in Scripture, exploring commentaries and theological treatises can be invaluable. These works often provide historical context, interpretive frameworks, and practical applications of biblical text.

3. **Online Courses and Workshops:** The digital age offers a multitude of learning opportunities. Online courses and workshops can offer structured and interactive ways to learn more about Christian ethics from scholars and practitioners around the globe.

4. **Community Discussion Groups:** Engaging with a community of believers can enrich your understanding of Christian ethics. Discussion groups, whether in-person or online, allow for the sharing of diverse perspectives, concerns, and insights.

5. **Conferences and Seminars:** Attending conferences and seminars on Christian ethics and related fields can be a way to stay informed on current discussions, research, and methodologies. It also offers the added benefit of connecting with individuals passionate about applying faith to everyday life.

The path towards integrating Christian moral principles into daily life is both challenging and rewarding. As you continue to seek wisdom and guidance, remember that you're part of a larger community striving towards the same goal.

Let the resources provided here serve as a starting point, but don't limit yourself. Be open to exploring new avenues of understanding, always ready to grow, adapt, and apply your faith in new and dynamic ways. Your journey in Christian ethics is as unique as your relationship with God – ongoing, deeply personal, and filled with endless opportunities for learning and transformation.

Resources for Further Study

In our journey through the complex and rich world of Christian ethics, we've traversed diverse terrains, from the foundational role of scripture and tradition in moral decision-making to the modern challenges posed by technology and globalization. It's crucial, however, to recognize that this book is but a gateway into the vast expanse of knowledge and wisdom that lies in studying Christian ethics more deeply. As we aim to navigate life's intricacies with a Christian lens, seeking resources for further study becomes essential.

Embarking on this path of deeper understanding, one might first look toward classic theological texts. The rich heritage of Christian ethics is illuminated within the writings of Augustine, Aquinas, and Bonhoeffer. Their works provide not just a historical perspective but a profound insight into the core of Christian moral philosophy, guiding us to reflect deeply on our ethical convictions.

To engage with Christian ethics is to continuously dialogue with scripture. Thus, a disciplined approach to Bible study, accompanied by esteemed biblical commentaries, is indispensable. Resources that merge scholarly rigor with accessibility, such as the works by N.T. Wright or Beth Moore, offer enriching perspectives that help contextualize ethical principles in our daily lives.

The intersection of faith and contemporary issues demands our attention now more than ever. Books and articles that tackle the ethical dimensions of technology, environmental stewardship, and social justice from a Christian viewpoint can equip us to address today's challenges effectively. Authors like Timothy Keller and Francis Schaeffer offer compelling narratives that encourage us to explore how our faith shapes our response to modern dilemmas.

As we consider the role of virtues in Christian ethics, engaging with philosophical traditions can elucidate the development of moral thought. Exploring works by Aristotle on virtue ethics, followed by contemporary interpretations from a Christian perspective by authors like Stan Hauerwas, can provide a deeper understanding of how virtues shape our character and actions.

One can't overlook the importance of community in ethical growth. Joining study groups, book clubs, or online forums dedicated to Christian ethics can offer new insights and foster a shared learning experience. Interaction within a community allows for questions to be raised, assumptions to be challenged, and ideas to be refined in light of collective wisdom.

In our endeavor to apply Christian ethics to daily decisions, practical guides and devotionals can serve as invaluable tools. They help integrate theological concepts into daily practices, transforming our understanding into actionable faith. Look for resources that offer daily reflections, prayers, and practical challenges.

The dynamic nature of moral philosophy means that new ethical issues continually emerge. Staying informed through reputable Christian ethics journals, podcasts, and websites can help bridge the gap between timeless principles and their application in an ever-changing world.

For those interested in a deeper theological and philosophical engagement, enrolling in courses or attending seminars that focus on Christian ethics can provide structured and comprehensive learning. Many universities and theological institutions offer programs tailored to various levels of interest and expertise.

Exploring the narratives of those who have walked the path of ethical resolution in their lives can also be enlightening. Biographies of notable Christians throughout history, who navigated ethical dilemmas with faith and integrity, offer inspiration and practical wisdom.

Conferences and workshops on Christian ethics present opportunities to engage directly with leaders in the field. These gatherings can be a source of cutting-edge thought, networking, and personal encouragement as we seek to apply our faith to the challenges of the day.

The role of art, literature, and film in exploring ethical themes should not be underestimated. Engaging with creative works that probe moral questions can stimulate our imagination and deepen our understanding in ways that academic texts may not.

In navigating the moral complexities of work, wealth, and stewardship, resources that provide a biblical perspective on these issues are crucial. Exploring how Christian ethics intersects with economic practices can influence how we approach our professional lives and financial decisions.

As we face the ethical considerations of marriage, family, and human life, it's vital to approach these topics with sensitivity and depth. Resources that explore these issues from a Christian standpoint can guide us through life's most intimate and challenging decisions.

Finally, the call to social justice and advocacy is an area where Christian ethics can dramatically impact the world around us. Seeking out resources that equip us for informed action can help translate our faith into effective engagement with societal issues.

As you continue on this journey, remember that the quest for deeper understanding and application of Christian ethics is a lifelong endeavor. Let these resources be your companions, guiding lights, and sources of inspiration as you seek to live out your faith in every aspect of your life.

9 781456 650155